I0413143

# Sedimentology and Reservoir Heterogeneity of a Valley-Fill Deposit—A Field Guide to the Dakota Sandstone of the San Rafael Swell, Utah

By Mark A. Kirschbaum and Christopher J. Schenk

Scientific Investigations Report 2010–5222

U.S. Department of the Interior
U.S. Geological Survey

**U.S. Department of the Interior**
KEN SALAZAR, Secretary

**U.S. Geological Survey**
Marcia K. McNutt, Director

U.S. Geological Survey, Reston, Virginia: 2011

For more information on the USGS—the Federal source for science about the Earth, its natural and living resources, natural hazards, and the environment, visit http://www.usgs.gov or call 1-888-ASK-USGS

For an overview of USGS information products, including maps, imagery, and publications, visit http://www.usgs.gov/pubprod

To order this and other USGS information products, visit http://store.usgs.gov

# Contents

# Figures

## Table

## Plate

## Conversion Factors

| Multiply | By | To obtain |
|---|---|---|
| inch (in) | 2.54 | centimeters (cm) |
| foot (ft) | 0.3048 | meter (m) |
| mile (mi) | 1.609 | kilometer (km) |

# Sedimentology and Reservoir Heterogeneity of a Valley-Fill Deposit—A Field Guide to the Dakota Sandstone of the San Rafael Swell, Utah

By Mark A. Kirschbaum and Christopher J. Schenk

## Abstract

Valley-fill deposits form a significant class of hydro-carbon reservoirs in many basins of the world. Maximizing recovery of fluids from these reservoirs requires an understanding of the scales of fluid-flow heterogeneity present within the valley-fill system.

The Upper Cretaceous Dakota Sandstone in the San Rafael Swell, Utah contains well exposed, relatively accessible outcrops that allow a unique view of the external geometry and internal complexity of a set of rocks interpreted to be deposits of an incised valley fill. These units can be traced on outcrop for tens of miles, and individual sandstone bodies are exposed in three dimensions because of modern erosion in side canyons in a semiarid setting and by exhumation of the overlying, easily erodible Mancos Shale.

The Dakota consists of two major units: (1) a lower amalgamated sandstone facies dominated by large-scale cross stratification with several individual sandstone bodies ranging in thickness from 8 to 28 feet, ranging in width from 115 to 150 feet, and having lengths as much as 5,000 feet, and (2) an upper facies composed of numerous mud-encased lenticular sandstones, dominated by ripple-scale lamination, in bedsets ranging in thickness from 5 to 12 feet. The lower facies is interpreted to be fluvial, probably of mainly braided stream origin that exhibits multiple incisions amalgamated into a complex sandstone body. The upper facies has lower energy, probably anastomosed channels encased within alluvial and coastal-plain floodplain sediments.

The Dakota valley-fill complex has multiple scales of heterogeneity that could affect fluid flow in similar oil and gas subsurface reservoirs. The largest scale heterogeneity is at the formation level, where the valley-fill complex is sealed within overlying and underlying units. Within the valley-fill complex, there are heterogeneities between individual sandstone bodies, and at the smallest scale, internal heterogeneities within the bodies themselves. These different scales of fluid-flow compartmentalization present a challenge to hydrocarbon exploration targeting paleovalley deposits, and producing fields containing these types of reservoirs may have significant bypassed pay, especially where well spacing is large.

## Introduction

There has been a large amount of study during the last few decades on incised valley-fill deposits (for example, Dalrymple and others, 1994), and on their potential as oil and gas reservoirs (for example, Dolson and others, 1991). Surprisingly few however, have well-documented examples showing the detailed heterogeneity within ancient valley fill successions. Even rarer are studies of valley fills that have large proportions of fluvial strata within them, as most have a significant proportion of estuarine facies.

This study gives an overview of the stratigraphy and sedimentology of the Upper Cretaceous Dakota Sandstone in the San Rafael Swell (fig. 1), provides a geologic field guide to well exposed units of the formation in outcrops on the west side of the San Rafael Swell in central Utah, and briefly discusses the succession as an analogue for similar type reservoirs.

The field guide explores relatively easy-to-access outcrops that show different scales of features ranging from lamination, beds, and individual sandstone bodies to genetic sequence. The strata are set within a time stratigraphic framework, and modern analogues help envision the ancient depositional environments. The field trip will be particularly useful to those trying to understand subsurface water and hydrocarbon reservoirs.

## Geologic Setting

Paleogeographic and isopach map reconstructions of the Cenomanian stratigraphic interval (fig. 2) represent about 5 million years (m.y.), between 93.5 and 98.5 Ma (time scale of Obradovich, 1993), and is almost the exact time frame represented by deposits of the Dakota Sandstone (fig. 3). The paleogeographic map shows an interpretation of a main trunk drainage system running parallel to the thrust front, although it may be that the Dakota deposits of this report were sourced directly from the Pavant thrust belt (DeCelles, 2004, his fig. 11), or at least, received sediment derived from the thrust

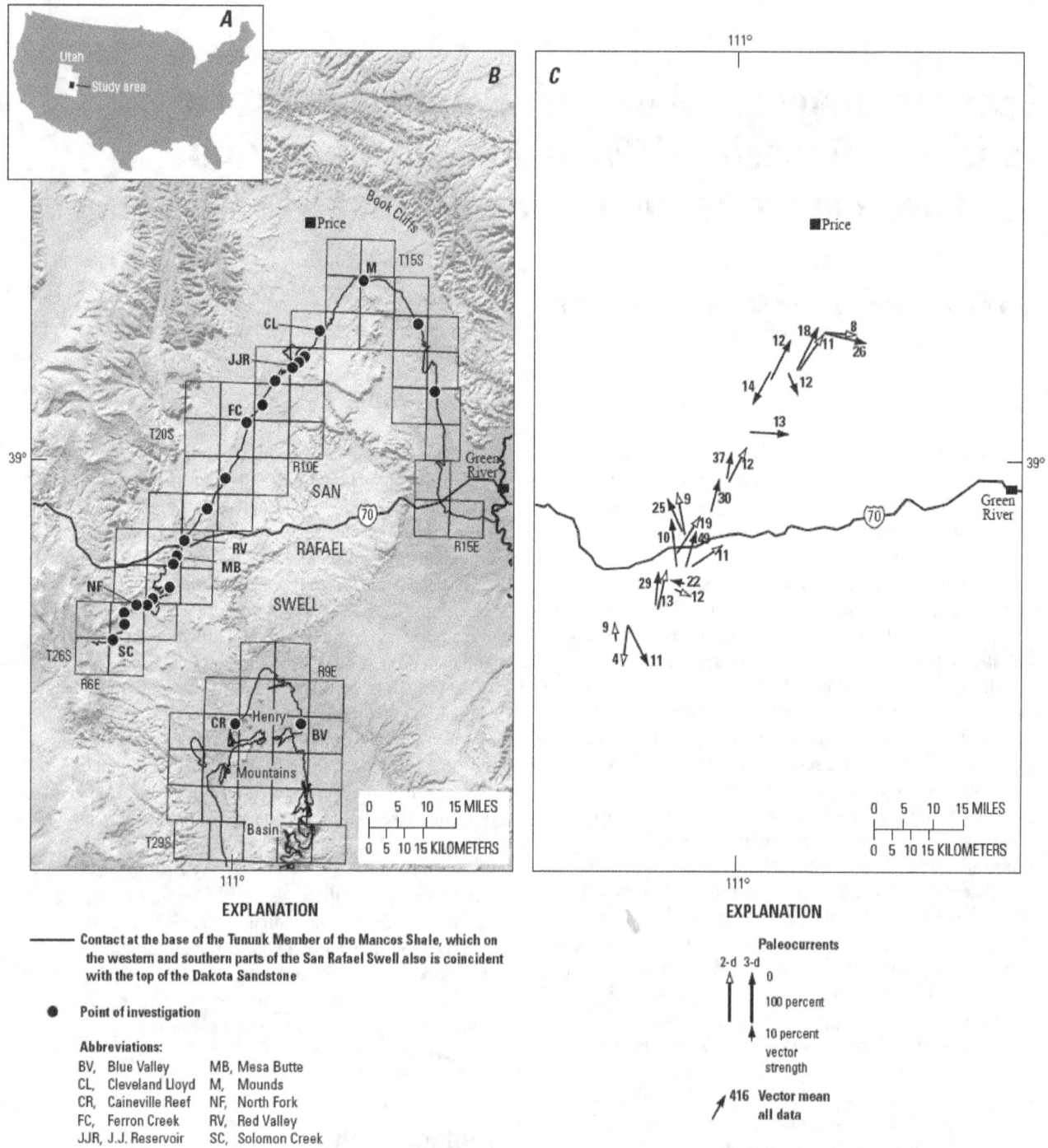

**Figure 1.** (*A*) Location of the study area in central Utah. (*B*) Location of points of investigation in the San Rafael Swell. (*C*) Distribution of paleocurrent measurements and calculated vector means taken from planar tabular (white arrows), trough (black arrows) cross stratification, and all measurements for the Dakota on the west side of the San Rafael Swell. The vector means were calculated using the method of Picard and Andersen (1975).

belt. The position of the thrust belt was about 100 miles west of the study area (fig. 2).

The modern San Rafael Swell is located on the edge of the ancient foredeep of the Cenomanian foreland basin as indicated by the thin area on the isopach map (fig. 2) and has been interpreted as a possible forebulge area (DeCelles, 2004). To the west, strata equivalent to the Dakota, the Sanpete Formation of the Indianola Group, thickens and coarsens in grain size, reflecting its proximity to the thrust belt (Lawton, 1985).

The size of the drainage basin that fed the Dakota fluvial system in the area of the San Rafael Swell is uncertain, but a reconstruction (fig. 4) shows a hypothetical drainage basin for the early Cenomanian using as an analogue the modern Pascagoula River drainage basin from the Gulf Coast of the United States in Mississippi.

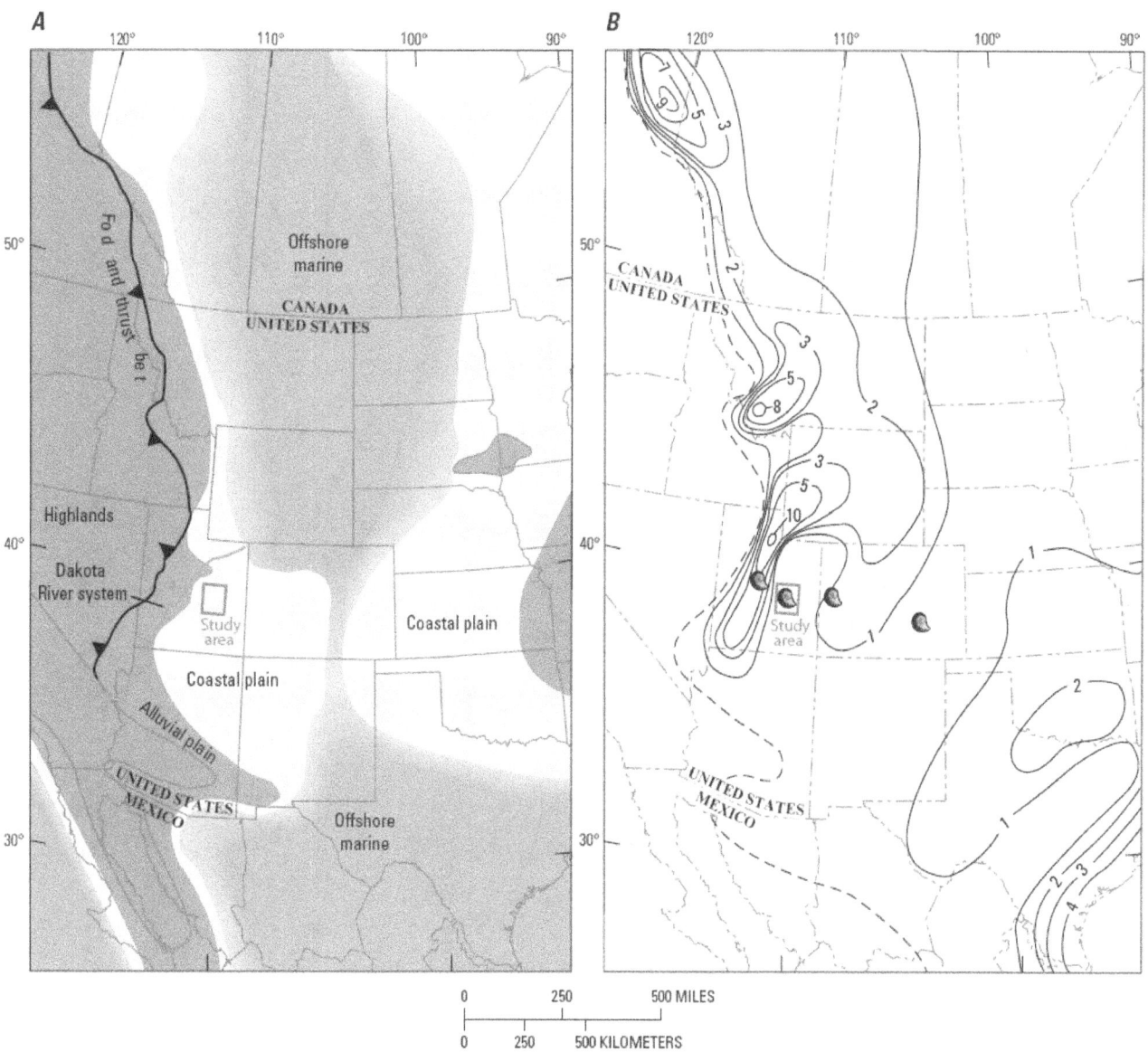

**Figure 2.**    (A) Paleogeography and (B) isopach of strata thickness (in hundreds of meters) for the Cenomanian Stage of the Late Cretaceous for middle North America (Roberts and Kirschbaum, 1995). The map interval represents the time period from about 98.5 to 93.5 Ma, based on radiometric dates by Obradovich (1993). Note the Cenomanian boundary is placed at 93.5 Ma at its upper boundary and at 99.6 Ma at its lower boundary (Cobban and others, 2006). Fault line marks the location of the restored thrust belt during Cenomanian time. Ammonite symbols on isopach map show the location of stratigraphic columns in figure 3.

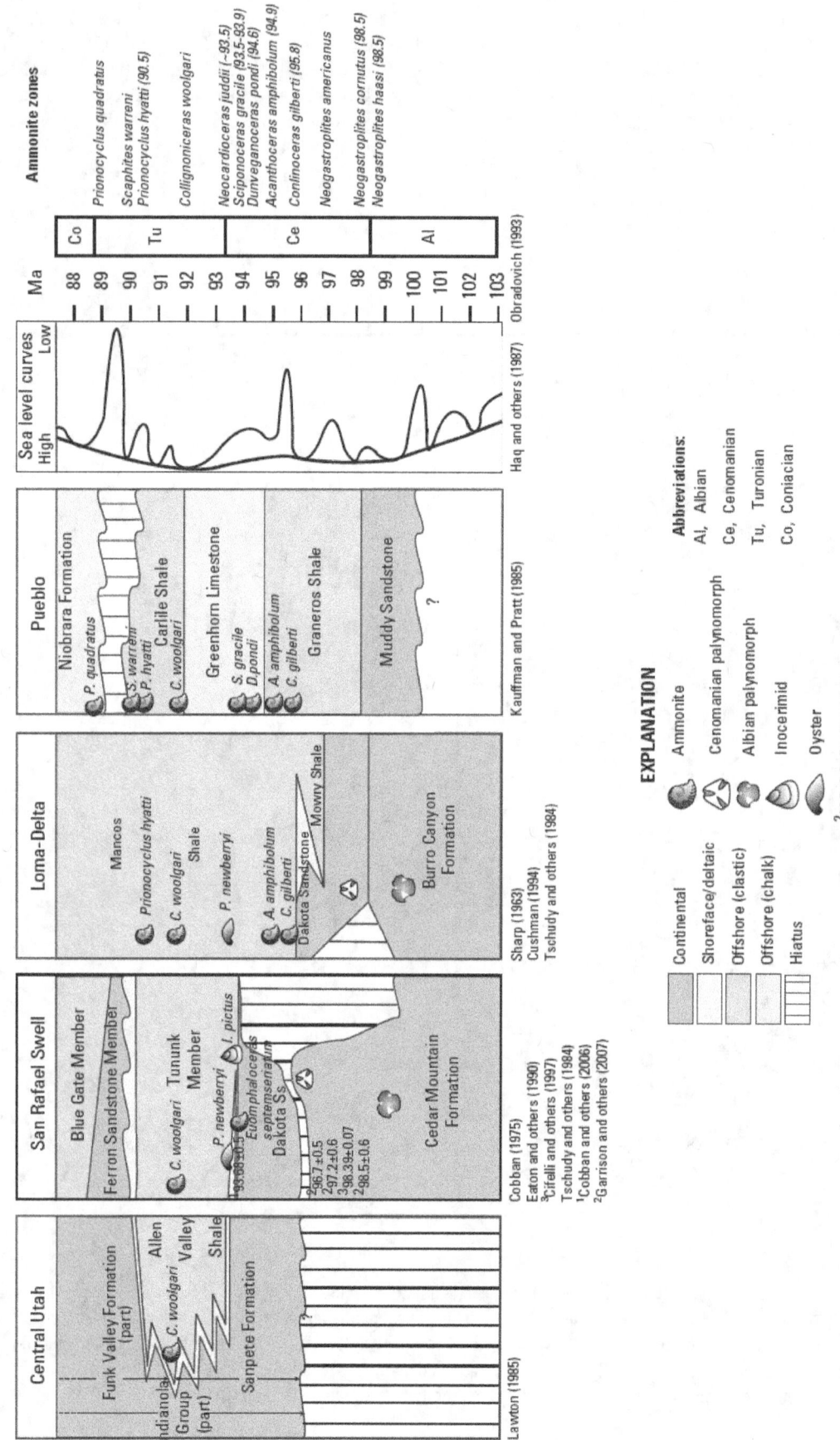

**Figure 3.** Columnar sections of stratigraphy and biostratigraphy for the mid-Cretaceous rocks on the San Rafael Swell and selected areas. For location of areas see figure 2.

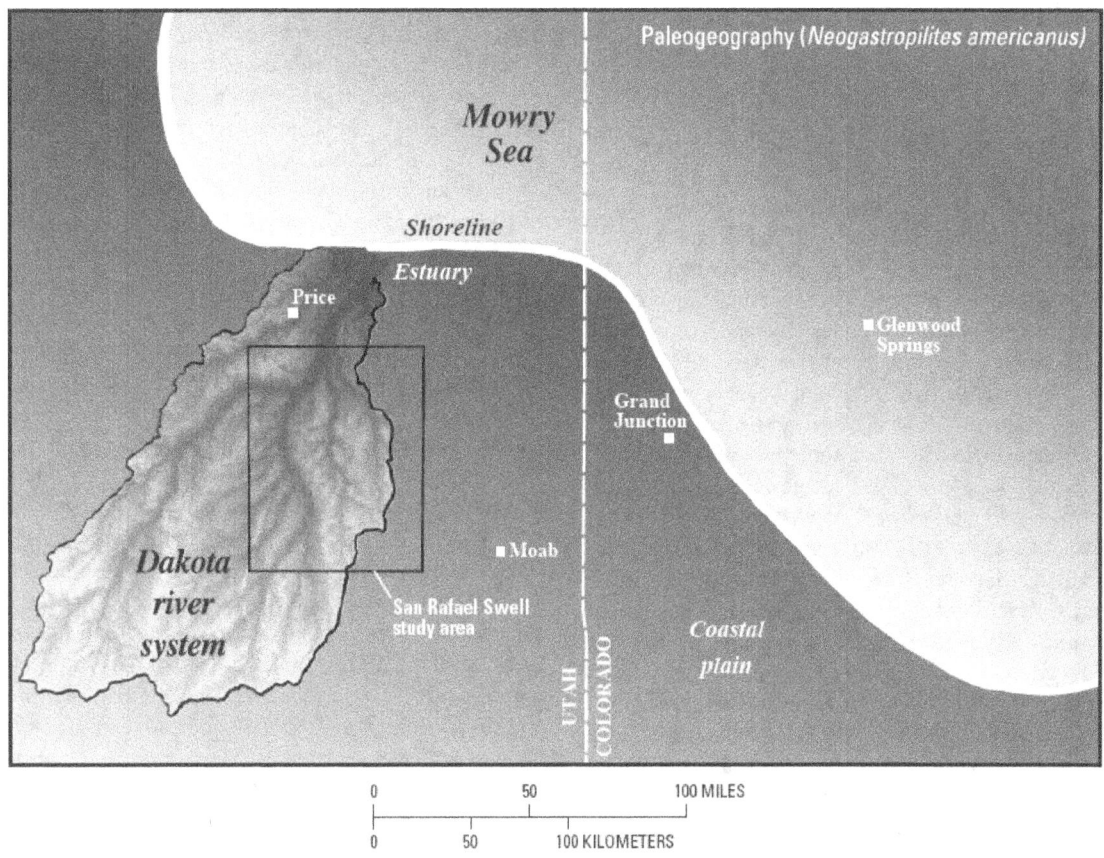

Figure 4.    Reconstruction of the paleogeography of the early Cenomanian sets the stage for the position of the shoreline near the end of deposition of the Cedar Mountain Formation. Shoreline position from Cobban and others (1994). During the 2-4.5 m.y. represented by the Dakota Sandstone, the shoreline would have migrated to the north to the position shown during the time of *Neogastropilites americanus*, and then eventually transgressed into the study area by the time of *Sciponoceras gracile* (see figure 3 for ammonite zones) and eventually overtopping the entire study area. The drainage basin of the modern Pascagoula River (dendritic shading) is superimposed on the study area to provide a relative scale of the Dakota system. Note that the Dakota Sandstone of the San Rafael Swell would represent just a tributary of that system.

# Stratigraphy and Age

## Cedar Mountain Formation

The Cedar Mountain Formation originally was named by Stokes (1944) for a succession of varicolored shale and lenticular sandstone and conglomerate beds in the northern San Rafael Swell (see fig. 5). Stokes (1952) subsequently included a basal conglomerate in the Cedar Mountain, the Buckhorn Conglomerate Member, and described the presence of carbonate nodules within the mudstone units. Kirkland and others (1997) break out several members within the Cedar Mountain. They describe two informal units that are in contact with the Dakota Sandstone, an uppermost Mussentuchit member of Cenomanian age and in some localities an older Ruby Ranch member partly of Albian age. Kirkland and others (1997) distinguished these two members by the presence of carbonate nodules in the Ruby Ranch member and smectitic mudstones in the Mussentuchit member. Northward in the vicinity of J.J. Reservoir (fig. 5), the smectitic unit contains conglomeratic sandstone at its base that extends over much of the northwestern and northeastern parts of the San Rafael Swell. At the type area of the Cedar Mountain near Buck-horn Reservoir, Stokes (1952, p. 1773) clearly included this conglomerate in the "Dakota" Formation and earlier Gilluly (1929, p. 119) called it Dakota (?). On the east side of the Swell, Young (1960, his fig. 6) called this conglomerate the upper Naturita sandstone, but called it middle Naturita sandstone on the west side of the Swell (Young, 1960, his fig. 15). Kirkland and others (1997) implied a Dakota name as well. It is our opinion that the conglomerate unit between the smectitic mudstone unit and the nodular carbonate mudstone unit is equivalent to the Mussentuchit member. The Dakota (that is, the Dakota valley-fill unit of this report) is only present on the west side of the Swell.

The age of the Cedar Mountain is late Albian to lower Cenomanian (fig. 3) based on dinosaur fossils, palynomorphs, and radiometric dates (Cifelli and others, 1997; Kirkland and others, 1997; Garrison and others, 2007). A minimum age of about 96 Ma is reported for the Cedar Mountain (Garrison and others, 2007).

## Dakota Sandstone

The unit we designate as the Dakota commonly has been called Dakota by previous workers (fig. 5). It was designated the upper Naturita sandstone of the Dakota Group by Young (1960, his fig. 15). The study unit within this report generally consists of: (1) a lower amalgamated fluvial sandstone facies, and (2) an upper deltaic/estuarine heterolithic facies. The lower unit is not present at the northernmost or eastern part of the Swell and is best represented on the southwestern part; it is best preserved in the Mesa Butte area (fig. 1). South of Interstate 70, the upper part of the Dakota contains as much as 19 feet (ft) of burrowed and hummocky bedded sandstone with some ball and pillow structures and symmetrical wave ripples, *Ophiomorpha* trace fossils, and marine bivalves indicating a lower shoreface origin for these sandstones (fig. 5, North Fork section). In the area around interstate 70 the unit contains fossils in the lower Tununk Member of the Mancos Shale ranging in age from latest Cenomanian to early Turonian (Eaton and others, 1990).

The age of the Dakota is constrained by Inoceramids and ammonites in the lowermost part of the Tununk Shale and by the dating of the Cedar Mountain Formation (fig. 3). The maximum age of the Dakota is based on radiometric dates in the Cedar Mountain, which range (using one sigma standard deviation) from 96.2 to 97.8 Ma. In the Mesa Butte area, the shoreface deposits at the top of the Dakota contain the ammonite *Euomphaloceras* (Kanabiceras) *septemseriatum* and *Pycnodonte newberryi*, both indicative of the late Cenomanian *Sciponoceras gracile* ammonite zone (Cobban, 1976), and various Inoceramids including *I. pictus* (Eaton and others, 1990). A bentonite from the zone of *E. septemseriatum* is dated at $93.68 \pm 0.5$ Ma by Cobban and others (2006) making a minimum age range of between about 93.2 and 94.2 Ma for the top of the Dakota. The range for deposition of the Dakota is therefore between about 2 and 4.5 m.y.

## Tununk Member of the Mancos Shale

The Tununk Member overlies the Dakota (figs. 3 and 5). It consists of gray silt and clay with minor sandstone and contains abundant marine Inoceramids and ammonites. In many places the contact with the Dakota is marked by a pebble lag composed of brown and gray chert and white quartzite pebbles and oysters (*Pycnodonte newberryi*) at or near the contact. In some localities the pebbles are matrix supported within a few feet of the contact. Eaton and others (1990) suggested this conglomerate, which can be as thick as 9 ft, to be the result of uplift and removal of basal Cedar Mountain sandstones; however, it is more likely related to reworking of the conglomerate at the base of the Mussentuchits member by marine wave ravinement.

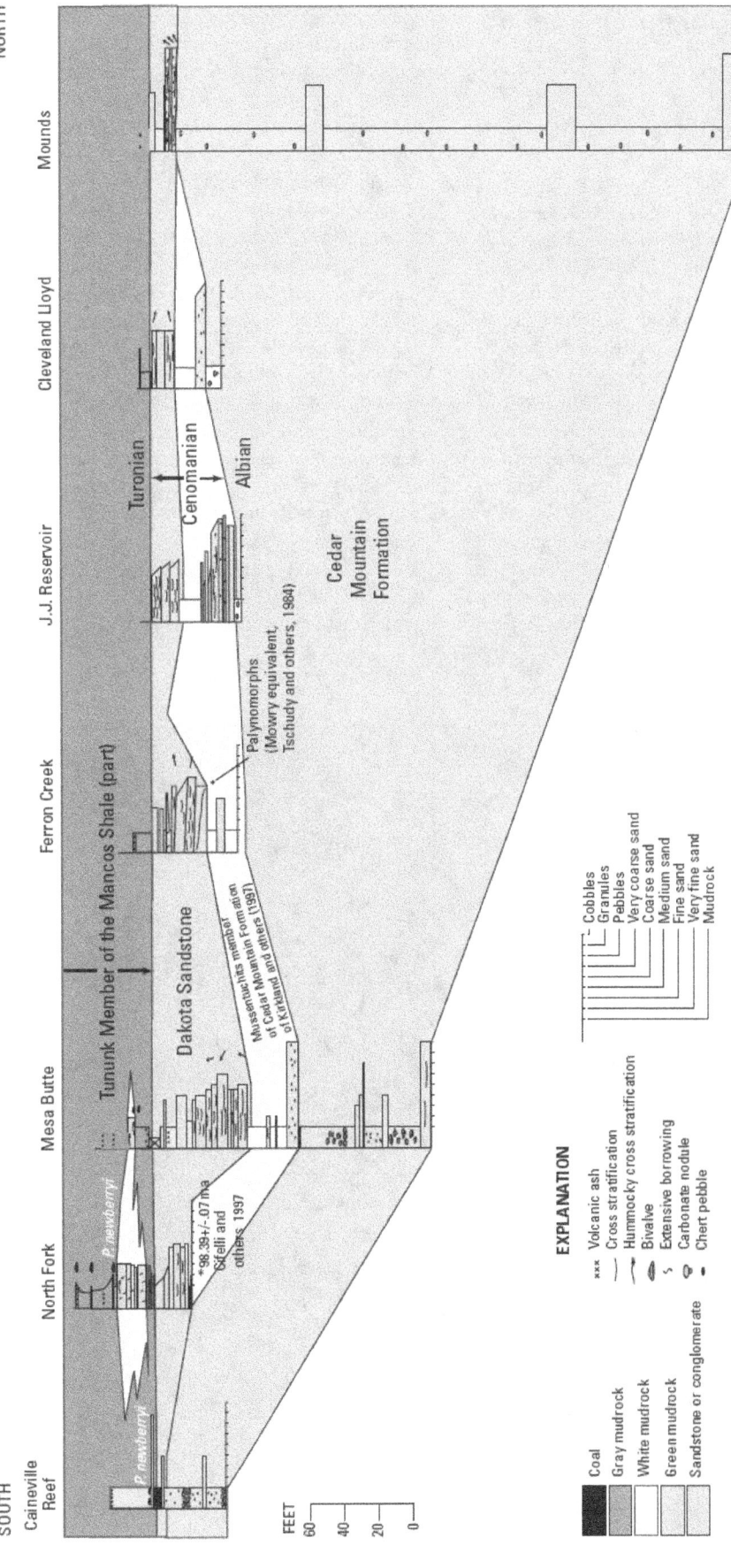

**Figure 5.** Cross section of the Cedar Mountain Formation, Dakota Sandstone, and part of the Tununk Member of the Mancos Shale on the west side of the San Rafael Swell and connected to southern part of the Swell at Caineville, Utah. Datum is the initial flooding surface at the top of the fluvial Dakota. Sections are located in figure 1B. Note the depositional thinning of the Cedar Mountain to the south and erosional truncation of the Mussentuchits member by the Dakota to the north. Cedar Mountain part of Mounds section modified from Young (1960).

# Facies Associations of the Dakota Sandstone

## Amalgamated Sandstone Unit

### Description

The amalgamated sandstone facies association consists of fine to very coarse sandstone, minor granular to pebbly sandstone, and minor mudrock and conglomerate (table 1). The facies association is as thick as about 70 ft and thins to zero in places. Internally, it can be characterized as consisting of multiple nested lenticular sandstone bodies dominated by large-scale cross stratification (fig. 6), but there also is a variety of lithofacies (table 1). The facies association contains distinct dipping accretion surfaces at some localities and, where the tops of bodies are exposed, the accretion surfaces display curved surfaces. In plan view (fig. 7), contacts between some bodies were observed to have intersecting erosional contacts and slightly sinuous traces. The overall width of the facies association is difficult to determine, but based on orientation of the outcrops and minor subsurface control (Henry

and Finn, 2003, their plate 1) the width could be as wide as about 8 miles (mi) or as narrow as about 5 mi. The facies association can be traced along depositional dip from Solomon Creek in the south to about Ferron Creek in the north, a distance of about 35 mi (fig. 1). Overall the paleocurrents of large scale trough and planar tabular cross stratification generally are to the north-northeast (fig. 1C). The main orientation of the unit generally is northward heading into the subsurface to the north along the San Rafael Swell (figs. 1, 5).

The facies association is best exposed and most easily accessible in the Mesa Butte area, just south of Interstate 70 (fig. 1). In this area, several sections were measured, including one complete detailed section (fig. 8), and numerous sketches were made from photomosaics (fig. 9) and then examined in the field. The main outcrop extends for about a mile in a direction about 10 degrees north of due east. Paleocurrent directions interpreted from large-scale cross stratification in the Mesa Butte area have a vector mean of 13 degrees based on 59 measurements (fig. 1C); therefore, the main outcrop is primarily oriented along depositional strike. Within the Mesa Butte study area, individual sandstone bodies are 8- to 28-ft thick and about 115- to 500-ft wide, based on a detailed examination of 6 sand bodies. The sandstone bodies have simple

**Figure 6.**  Large-scale cross stratification in the lower part of the Dakota Sandstone near Mesa Butte (photograph courtesy of Steve Cumella, Bill Barrett Corporation).

external shapes with a lack of overbank extensions referred to in some reports as wings. Reincison into older sand bodies is common and scours cut 10 to 15 ft into older units. The main complex at Mesa Butte thins rapidly to the west (fig. 9), but then thickens again to about 55 ft in the westernmost exposure before heading into the subsurface (fig. 7).

Internally, the lower interval consists of seven facies (table 1), but it is dominated by cross stratification (fig. 8). Multiple scours reduce most cross beds to less than a foot in

thickness, although large-scale cross stratification is common with heights of 2 to 3 ft. Cross stratification commonly contain prominent reactivation surfaces (fig. 5). Ripple laminated sandstone is less common, but is abundant at some locations, predominantly near the tops of sandstone bodies, and it can have both sub- and super-critical angles of climb (fig. 10A, B). Convolute bedding, horizontal lamination (fig. 10D) and scour features (fig. 10C) filled with sandstone are present locally within the unit.

**Table 1.** Lithofacies of the lower and upper parts of the Dakota Sandstone from the San Rafael Swell and Blue Valley area, Utah.

| Facies | Description of sedimentary structures | Grain size | Thickness of facies unit | Comments |
|---|---|---|---|---|
| Upper Dakota: lenticular sandstone and mudrock unit | | | | |
| Cross-stratified sandstone | Trough and planar-tabular cross stratification; 0.5 to 1.6 ft beds; local convoluted beds to 5 ft; ripups common | Fine to medium | 12 ft | Dominantly planar tabular; one set with counter-current ripples; small troughs up to 1 ft wide; possible antidunes. |
| Asymmetrical rippled sandstone | Dominant sedimentary structure in sandstones; minor ripup clasts | Fine to medium; minor coarse or granules | 4.3–12 ft | Associated with lateral accretion surfaces; some inclined heterolithic. |
| Symmetrical rippled sandstone | | Very fine to fine | <1.0 ft | |
| Laminated sandstone | Horizonal to crude laminations | Very fine to fine | 0.8 to 4.3 ft | Plant fragments contains oysters (*Crassostrea*?). |
| Burrowed sandstone | Some *Ophiomorpha*; *Skolithos*? | | 0.8 to 15 ft | |
| Mudrock | Claystone to sandy siltstone | | 0.9 to 17 ft | |
| Carbonaceous shale | Laminated dark-gray clay to silt-shale | | 0.5 to 12 ft | Root traces common. |
| Coal | | | 0.4 to 0.8 ft | |
| Lower Dakota: amalgamated sandstone unit | | | | |
| Intraformational conglomerate | Clay and siltstone clasts; some fossilized wood | Granules to cobbles | | Common on basal contacts. |
| Extraformational conglomerate | Gray, black, and light-brown chert, and minor white quartzite | Granules to pebbles | Up to 11 ft | More common in southernmost sections south of Mesa Butte, but still present throughout area. |
| Crossbedded sandstone | Trough and planar-tabular cross stratification; individual beds 0.2 to 4 ft thick | Upper fine to granule | Bedsets up to 10 ft | Reactivation surfaces common, well rounded grains; local carbonaceous fragments; widths of troughs 1.5 to 6 ft. |
| Horizontally laminated sandstone | | Fine to medium | 0.3 to 3 ft | Upper flow regime, locally filling scour holes. |
| Rippled sandstone | Low- to high-angle climb | Very fine to fine | 0.3 to 2 ft | Minor component of this facies association. |
| Convoluted sandstone | | Fine to coarse | 0.6 to 3.6 ft | |
| Mudrock | | | 0.1 to 0.4 ft | |

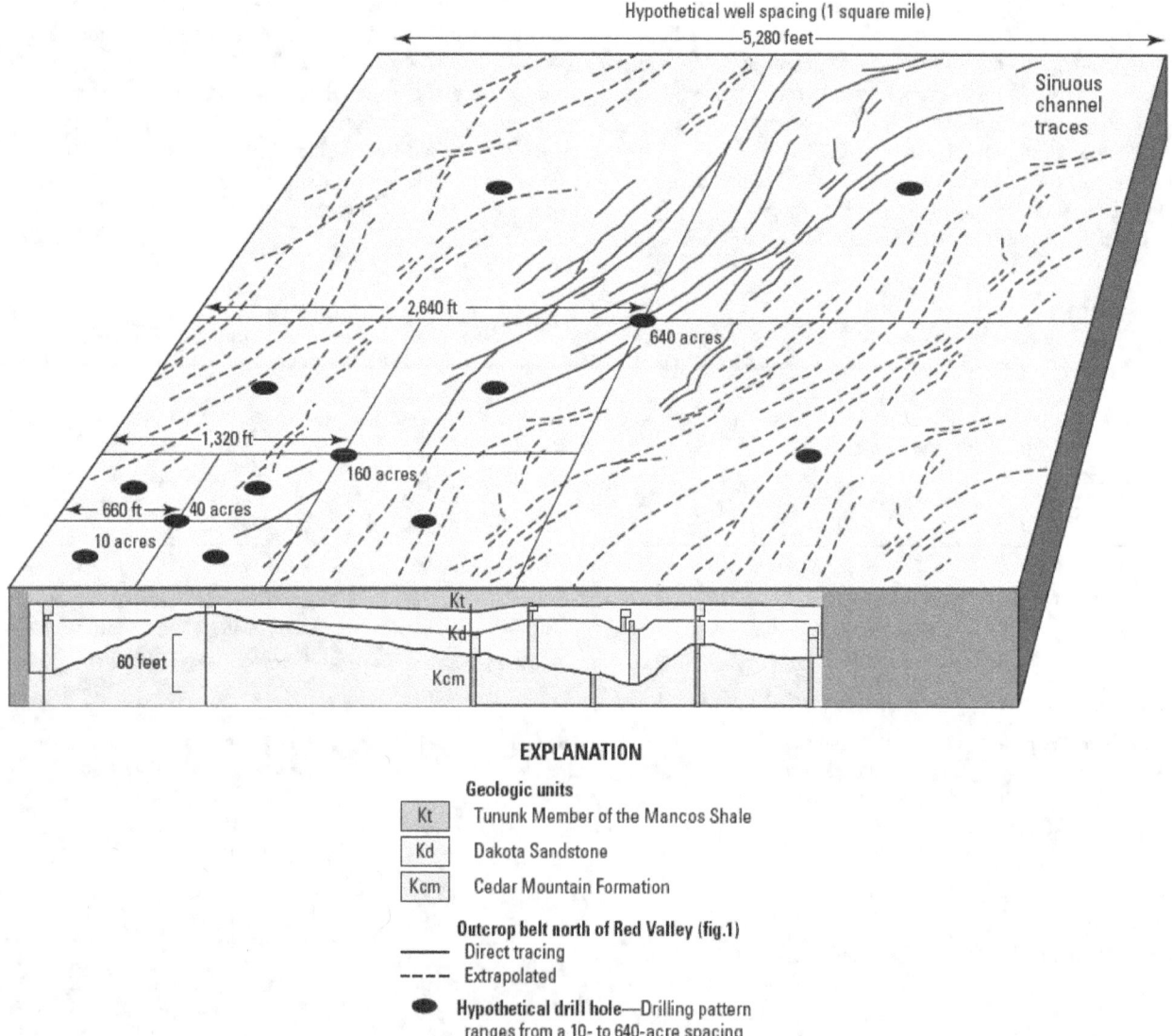

**EXPLANATION**

**Geologic units**

| Kt | Tununk Member of the Mancos Shale |

| Kd | Dakota Sandstone |

| Kcm | Cedar Mountain Formation |

**Outcrop belt north of Red Valley (fig.1)**
—— Direct tracing
- - - - Extrapolated

● Hypothetical drill hole—Drilling pattern
ranges from a 10- to 640-acre spacing

**Figure 7.** Valley-fill deposits within a square-mile area. The top view is a tracing from an aerial photograph of the outcrop belt north of Red Valley (see fig. 1 for location) showing exhumed channel forms in the resistant Dakota Sandstone. The front cross sectional view shows the general thickness of the Dakota valley fill as measured in the main side canyon east of Mesa Butte (Stop 1 of the field trip). Horizontal distance of cross section is about 0.75 mile.

**Figure 8.** Measured section of the lower and upper parts of the Dakota Sandstone in the Mesa Butte area. Sedimentary structures are indicated in margin of section. The section was measured in the main side canyon and its location is shown on the far left (west) section on plate 1. Also shown in figure 9 and figure 15*B* (measured section 9). Note the lower part of the section (lower facies association) is dominated by cross stratification and the upper part of the section (upper facies association) is dominated by ripple lamination.

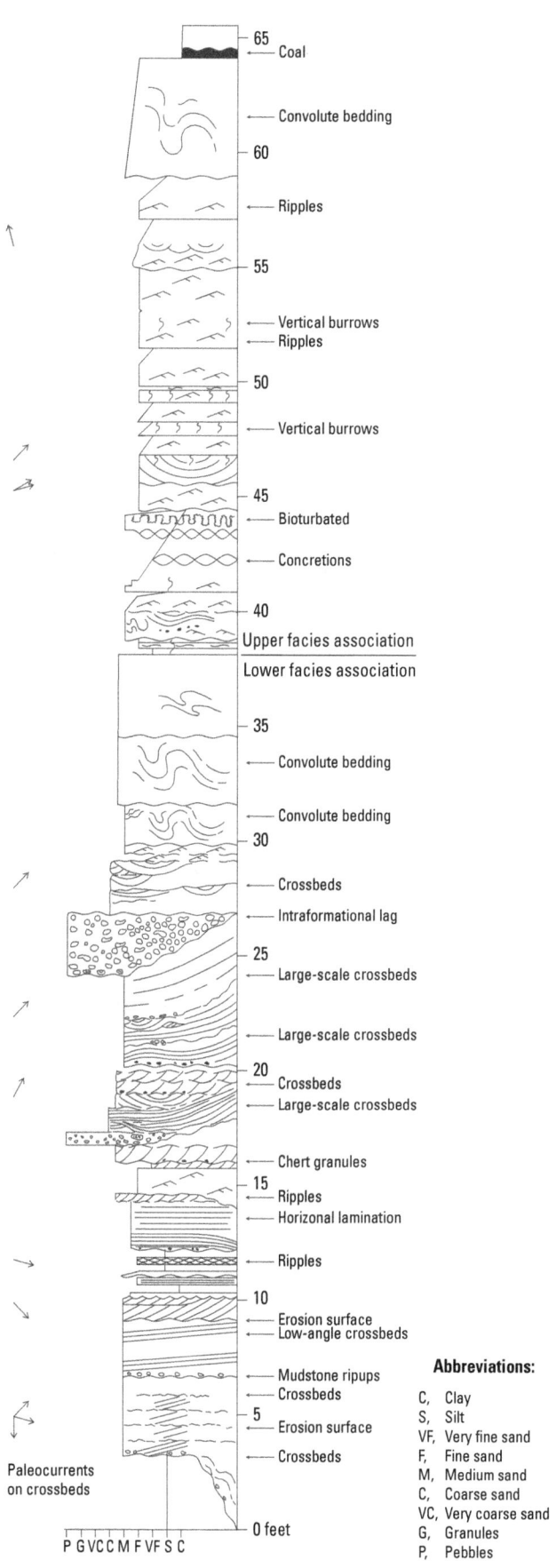

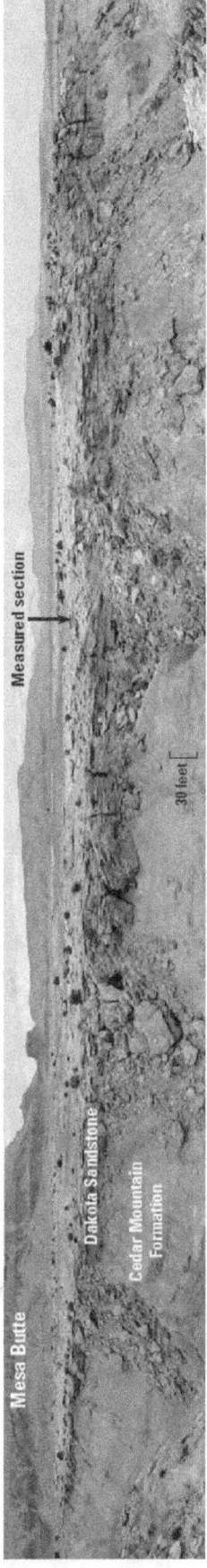

**Figure 9.** Photomosaic of the Dakota Sandstone on the north side of the main side canyon of Muddy Creek east of the Mesa Butte area. View is toward the northwest (photographs courtesy of Steve Cumella, Bill Barrett Corporation). Details of measured section shown on figure 8.

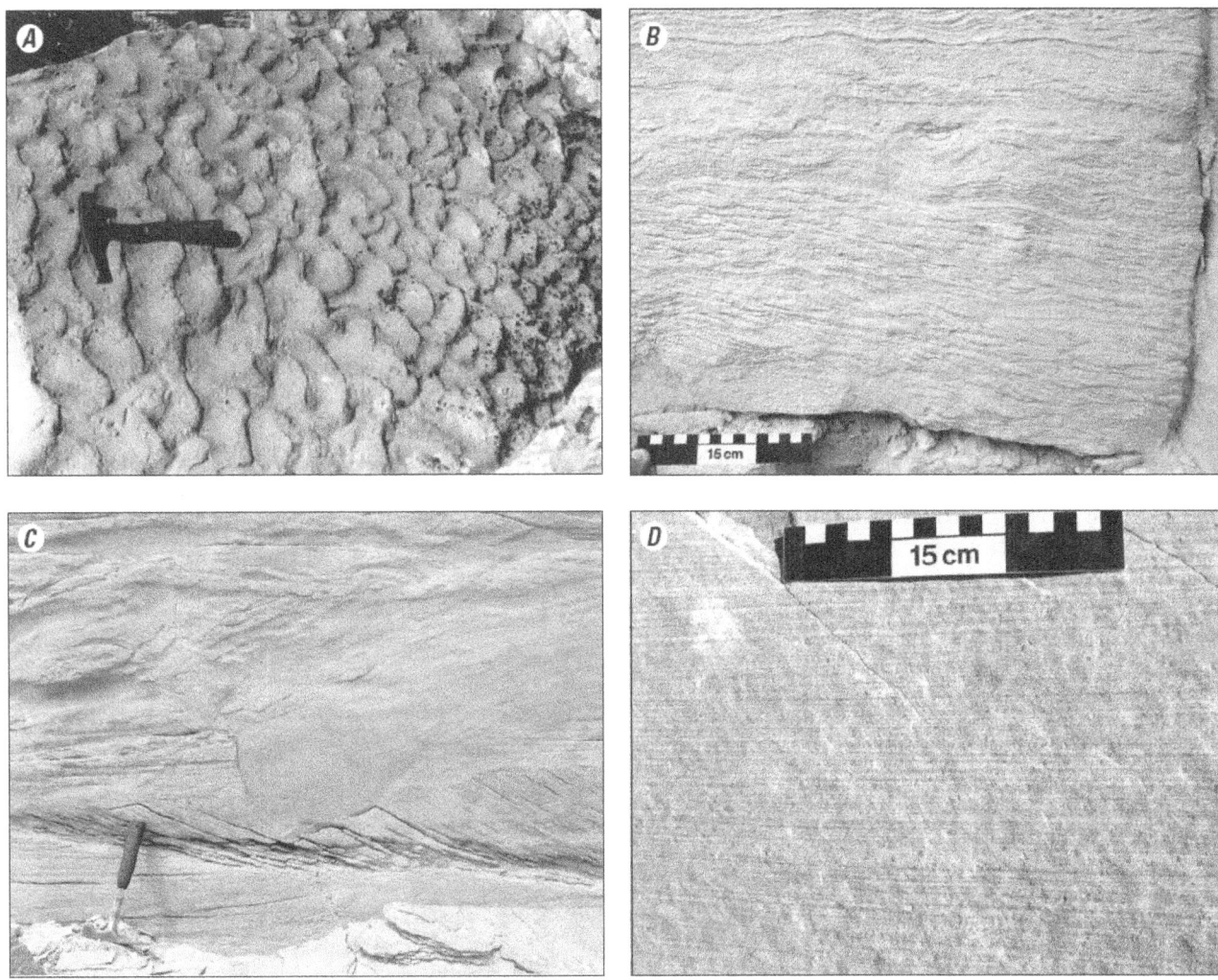

**Figure 10.**    Typical sedimentary structures in the lower facies association of the Dakota Sandstone. (*A*) Linguoid ripples formed on top of a bed; flow to right. Hammer for scale. Location is south of the J.J. Reservoir measured section (see figs. 1, 5). (*B*) Climbing ripples with sub- to super-critical angles of climb in the Mesa Butte area. (*C*) Trough cross-stratification scoured and overlain by subhorizontal lamination, which in turn is eroded by a scour pit; location is south of the J.J. Reservoir measured section. (*D*) Horizontal lamination produced by upper flow regime plane bed from about the 13-ft level in the Mesa Butte measured section (fig. 8).

## Interpretation

The complex sand body geometry and lateral thickness variability of this facies association is interpreted to result from being deposited in a confined valley, incised during the middle to late Cenomanian. The interpretation of a valley is supported by the differential erosion into the Cedar Mountain with respect to a marker bed in the Cedar Mountain and on the lack of interfingering between the Dakota channels and Cedar Mountain mudstone (fig. 7). The individual sand bodies are interpreted as fluvial channels based on their overall upward decrease in flow strength that can be observed in the few cases where sand bodies have not been truncated by a younger body (fig. 8). The amalgamation of the channels is due to generally low accommodation space available to channels confined in a valley. The presence of dinosaur footprints in sand bodies near the base of the Dakota confirms that the individual sand bodies are the active channels with depths of less than 28 ft rather than the entire Dakota being the channel with depths as much as 75 ft, because the footprints imply subaerial exposure. Lateral accretion surfaces indicate some bank-attached bars, but it is not clear exactly what type of rivers produced these deposits. Multiple episodes of incision within individual channels are indicated by truncation of cross beds leaving only inches of preserved sets especially in the bottom of the bodies. However, the large preserved crossbeds (fig. 6) indicates that large two-dimensional barforms were present with multiple reactivation surfaces indicating episodic flow with little preservation of suspended load, which might be suspected in braided streams or bank attached bars (fig. 11A). Scour holes may be indicative of channel confluences (Ashmore and Parker, 1983), and they point to active multiple channels, which is more indicative of braided than meandering streams (fig. 10C).

## Lenticular Sandstone and Mudrock Unit

### Description

This facies association consists of interbedded lenticular sandstone and mudrock with eight lithofacies (table 1). The most distinctive feature is the presence of sandstone bodies generally 5 to 6 ft thick but can be as much as 12 ft thick, and of short lateral extent (less than about 50 ft) that are enclosed within heterolithic deposits (plate 1). Sandstone is fine to medium grained and predominantly ripple laminated, although the unit has various types of sedimentary structures (fig. 12, table 1). The sandstone bodies have prominent accretion surfaces, and in the Mesa Butte area, they dip as much as 27 degrees, but mostly range from 14 to 25 degrees in their steepest parts based on about 15 measurements of accretion surfaces. Paleoflow is oblique and perpendicular to the accretion surfaces based on measurements observed for ripples. Surfaces shallow to a few degrees at their lower boundary. Accretion surfaces form bedsets whose basal surfaces have eroded older accretion bedsets. Paleocurrents within the bodies

show a wide dispersion of transport, but are within a single quadrant of the compass, indicating an overall unimodal distribution. One sandstone body, in the Mesa Butte area, is about 30-ft wide and can be walked out in a slightly sinuous path for about 200 ft. The bodies are clearly sinuous in form and exhumed bodies can be seen on tracings from aerial photographs (fig. 7); paleocurrent indicates paleoflow was mainly in a northerly direction (fig. 1C). In a depositional downdip direction, the channel forms have considerable mud and carbonaceous debris interbedded with sandstone, and the channel fill can be described as inclined heterolithic strata.

Other lithologies within the facies association include burrowed sandstone, minor amounts of carbonaceous shale and coal, and oyster beds (table 1). Fossils from the mudrock units include leaves and brackish water bivalves, and the mudrock commonly is root penetrated. Thin coal beds are most common in the thinner part of the sections presumably near the edges of the valley margins.

### Interpretation

This facies association was deposited in several different depositional environments. The presence of minor coal, carbonaceous shale, and leaf fossils indicates freshwater influence, whereas the presence of brackish water bivalves and oysters indicate marine or tidal influence. Symmetrical ripples indicate wave influence as well.

The sandstone bodies are interpreted to be channel deposits because of their overall fining upward grain size indicating decrease in flow strength upward. The lateral accretion surfaces and sinuous form of the channels indicate meandering; however, the narrow width of the channels indicates that they were short lived—that is, they did not meander widely. Multiple scours within the accretion sets probably indicate major floods and reorientation of the channels. This seems to indicate (1) higher flows during floods producing cross bedded units, and (2) primarily lower flow regimes during lower flows as seen by the dominance of ripples. The distinction between this facies association and the underlying amalgamated sandstone facies association is not always apparent. Because of the localized nature of preservation of this facies association, these types of lower-energy deposits also are present on the edges of some of the higher energy deposits. This facies association is similar to those described for a bayhead delta complex for the Neslen Formation in central Utah (Kirschbaum and Hettinger, 2004) or an anastomosed stream complex in the Dakota Sandstone in southern Utah (Kirschbaum and McCabe, 1992).

A possible modern analogue would be the bayhead deltaic system in the Pascagoula River, Mississippi (fig. 11B), in which a valley was cut during the last glacial maximum and lowered sea level, and then was flooded during the subsequent melting of the ice (Kindinger and others, 1994). Today, the river is building into the estuary of the flooded valley. Updip from the estuarine facies are multiple anastomosing channels within a wetland. A logical interpretation for the location of

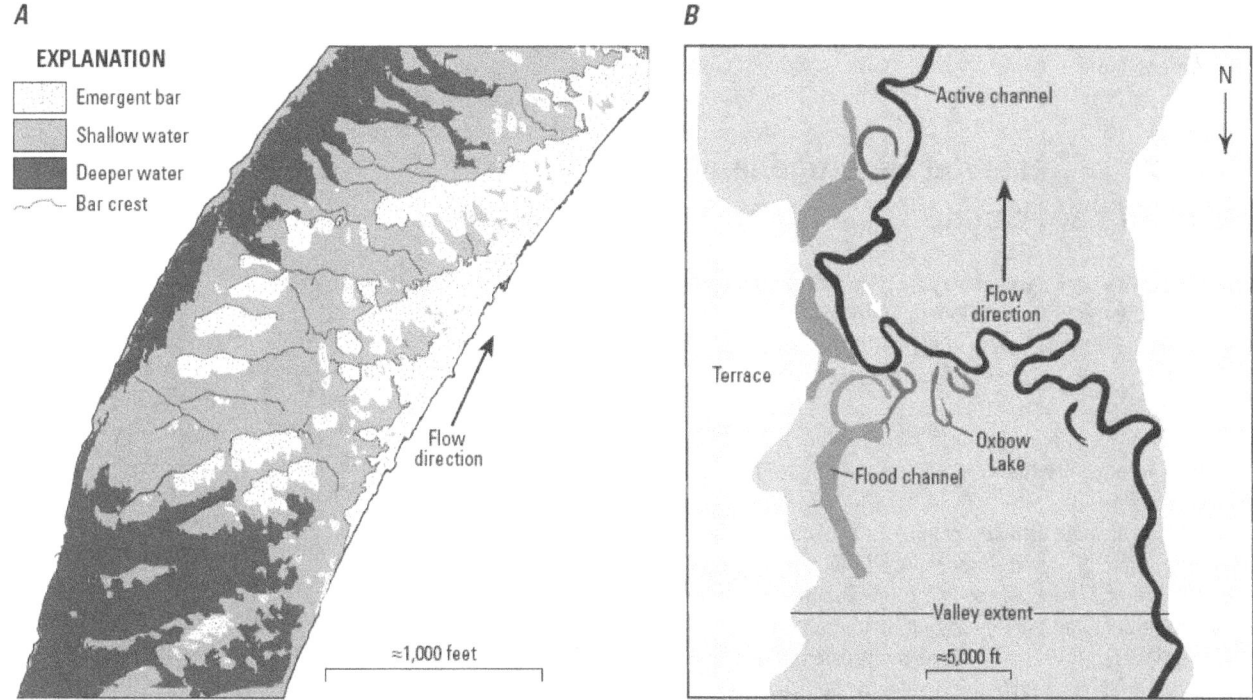

**Figure 11.** (*A*) Tracing of a channel and barforms from a tributary of the Orinoco River in South America. Side-attached transverse bars are a possible analogue for the large-scale cross stratification in the lower facies of the Dakota Sandstone at Mesa Butte. (*B*) Tracing of the lower reaches of the modern Pascagoula River in Mississippi about 16 miles upstream from the river's mouth where low gradient, highly sinuous channels are confined to an incised valley. Note that some parts of the channel of the Pascagoula River curve back (small arrow) upstream, a pattern that is similarly envisioned for some of the small channels of the upper facies of the Dakota at Red Valley (Stop 2).

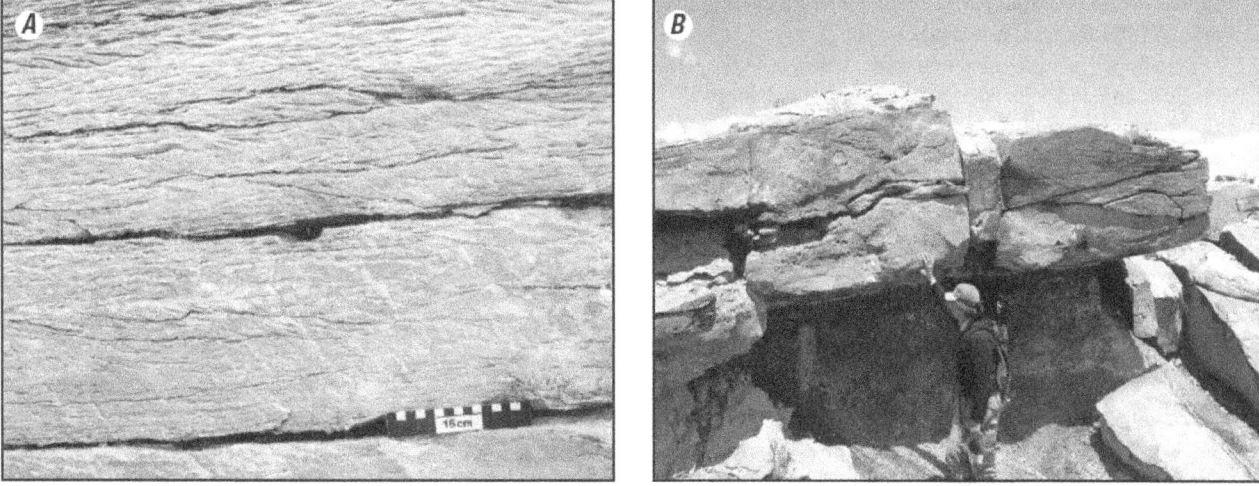

**Figure 12.** Sedimentary structures in the upper facies association of the Dakota Sandstone. (*A*) Ripple lamination. (*B*) Trough cross stratification and mud chip conglomerate (pockmarks near geologist hand).

the coals in the upper parts of paleovalleys is that they developed on interfluves during relative sea-level rise when water tables were rising.

# Overview of Reservoir Heterogeneity of the Dakota Sandstone

The various scales of heterogeneity in valley-fill deposits present a challenge to explorationists not only in the determination of the overall geometry of the valley fill but also with significant bypassed pay that arises where well spacing is large compared to the geometry of the sandstones within the valley fill. The valley-fill complex in the Dakota exhibits several scales of heterogeneity that could affect fluid flow in similar subsurface reservoirs.

The largest scale of heterogeneity is a function of the variability in lateral extent of the valley-fill complex, which is sealed within mudstones of the overlying Tununk Member of the Mancos Shale and the underlying bentonitic mudstones of the Cedar Mountain Formation. The next scale of heterogeneity is related to the amalgamated sandstone bodies within the valley-fill complex, where the sandstones are multistory and multilateral bodies that potentially could form individual reservoir compartments. Contacts between the individual channel bodies are erosional and might create permeability differences between sandstone bodies as noted by Willis (1998).

The next scale of heterogeneity is within the individual sandstone bodies, as grain size, lithology, type of physical and biogenic sedimentary structures, and diagenesis are factors controlling variations in fluid flow at this scale (Willis, 1998, his figs. 14*G* and 15; Willis and White, 2000; Pranter and others, 2007). Sedimentary structures cause directional permeability that varies from bed to bed, and diagenetic barriers may create significant local porosity and permeability variations (Willis and White, 2000). Thin shale units adjacent to sandstones create potential barriers that could affect vertical migration of fluids (Pranter and others, 2007).

In the upper facies association of the valley-fill complex, sandstone channels are isolated mostly within mudstones creating compartmentalization of the sandstone bodies. Lateral accretion surfaces create potential barriers within the sandstones (Pranter and others, 2007) particularly where a heterolithic fill is present, which is common in the Dakota Sandstone.

# Field Trip Stop Descriptions

This field guide has been developed from exposures of the San Rafael Swell (fig. 13), using the following criteria: (1) good exposures, (2) a variety of sand-body geometries and sedimentary structures, and (3) ready access to outcrops. The first two stops do require several long walks to the best exposures.

The field trip ideally would start and finish at Green River, Utah and the complete trip would require a day and a half—one day on the west side of the San Rafael Swell and one half day in the southern part of the Swell (fig. 13). An alternate trip can be completed in a single day by restricting visits to Stops 1.1, 1.2, 1.4, 3, and 4 while also passing through the scenic Capitol Reef National Park (fig. 13).

## Stop 1    Mesa Butte Area

The Mesa Butte area is located about 60 miles west of Green River, Utah or about 45 miles east of Salina, Utah on the west side of the San Rafael Swell south of Exit 99 along I-70 (fig. 13). The first few stops are within the Mesa Butte 7.5-minute topographic quadrangle in sec. 25, T. 23 S., R. 6 E.

Take Exit 99 and turn south on the two track dirt road (called Blue Road to the south and County Road 912 to the north). Proceed south about 1 mile on the dirt track. The road curves to the west into section 26 into a side tributary of Muddy Creek. Note the thin coal near the top of the Dakota Sandstone. Continue on into section 25 and park the vehicle in the southwestern part of the northwest quarter of section 25 (fig. 14). You should park near the head of the small side drainage of the main canyon. Note: The two-track road is on bentonitic shale of the Tununk Member of the Mancos Shale and is impassable when wet.

## Stop 1.1    Side Canyon of Muddy Creek, East of Mesa Butte

Access to Stop 1.1 requires a hike of moderate difficulty to the south side of the drainage, which is an east-oriented side canyon to Muddy Creek (fig. 14). Initially walk due east avoiding the small north-oriented subsidiary drainage before angling to the northeast. The best views are in the morning or early afternoon.

## Objectives

This stop provides an overview of the stratigraphy of the Dakota Sandstone and adjacent units, and a view of the internal architecture of the Dakota Sandstone.

## Discussion

The Dakota Sandstone is overlain by marine shale of the Tununk Member of the Mancos Shale and is in turn overlain by the Ferron Sandstone Member of the Mancos Shale, which supports the cliffs of Mesa Butte to the west and the Coal Cliffs to the northwest. The Dakota is underlain by the alluvial bentonitic mudrock of the Cedar Mountain Formation (Garrison and others, 2007). The exact contact between members of the Cedar Mountain is uncertain, but there is an overall change from carbonate nodules within the Ruby Ranch member

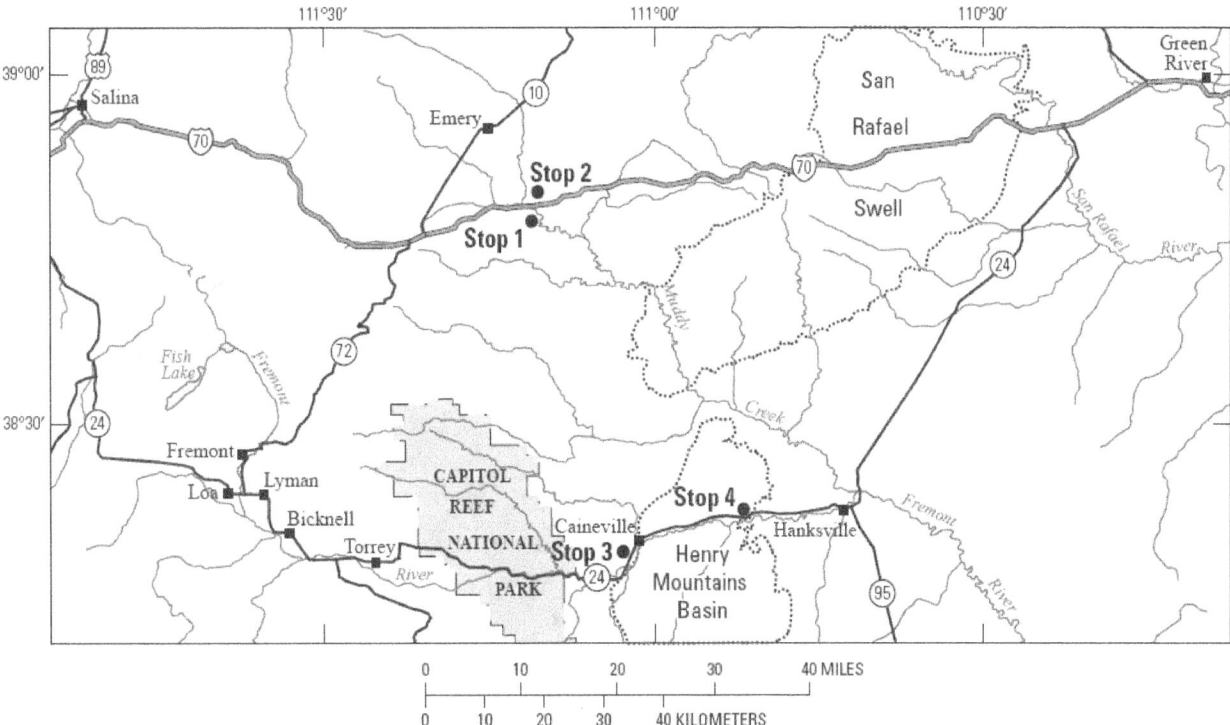

**Figure 13.** Locations of stops for the field trip.

and the overlying bentonitic mudrock of the Mussentuchits member of the Cedar Mountain.

The Dakota Sandstone is dominated by amalgamated sandstone bodies in the lower part of the exposure and smaller ribbon sandstone bodies encased in mudrock in the upper part (fig. 15, *plate 1*). The sandstone bodies have erosional bases and are composed mainly of small- to large-scale cross stratification (fig. 15D).

A hierarchy of erosion surfaces can be observed within the outcrop—master erosion surfaces at the base (fluvial incision) and top (marine transgressive) and numerous internal fluvial erosion surfaces (fig. 15 and *plate 1*). Considering that the succession was deposited over at least 2 m.y., the internal erosion surfaces could reflect reincision of drainages following repeated falls in sea level (fig. 3) or reworking by avulsive events in an overall low accommodation setting. Notice the lack of overbank deposits—the channel bodies are relatively simple without wings. The widths of individual sand bodies are from about 115 to 500 ft, which is similar to the open channels (about 300 ft) in the field of view in figure 11, but from a slightly different depositional environment. Overall, the sand bodies appear to be confined to their channels and lack preserved overbank deposits.

## Reservoir Considerations

This location is particularly enlightening in terms of the overall geometry of the Dakota sandstone bodies and their internal complexity. At this stop, you have an unobstructed view of almost a mile of outcrop and can observe a formation thickness change from about 5 to 70 ft (figs. 9, 15; *plate 1*). The tendency is to focus one's attention on the sandstone, and most visitors tend to comment on the overall continuity of the sandstone unit. This continuity is illustrated by examining figure 15A where the generalized section outlines a simple form of the Dakota. This generalized cross sectional view is similar to many modern and ancient cross sections of valley fill successions for its simplicity; however, a closer look at the internal geometry based on mapping internal erosion surfaces reveals extreme discontinuity and compartmentalization (fig. 15B and C; *plate 1*). The sandstone bodies are mostly in direct contact with other bodies, but it is not clear what the transmissivity would be between them because of possible permeability differences. There also are minor mudrock intervals that could be potential barriers to flow. The interval is situated between marine shale above and bentonitic mudrock below, thus providing good top and bottom seals.

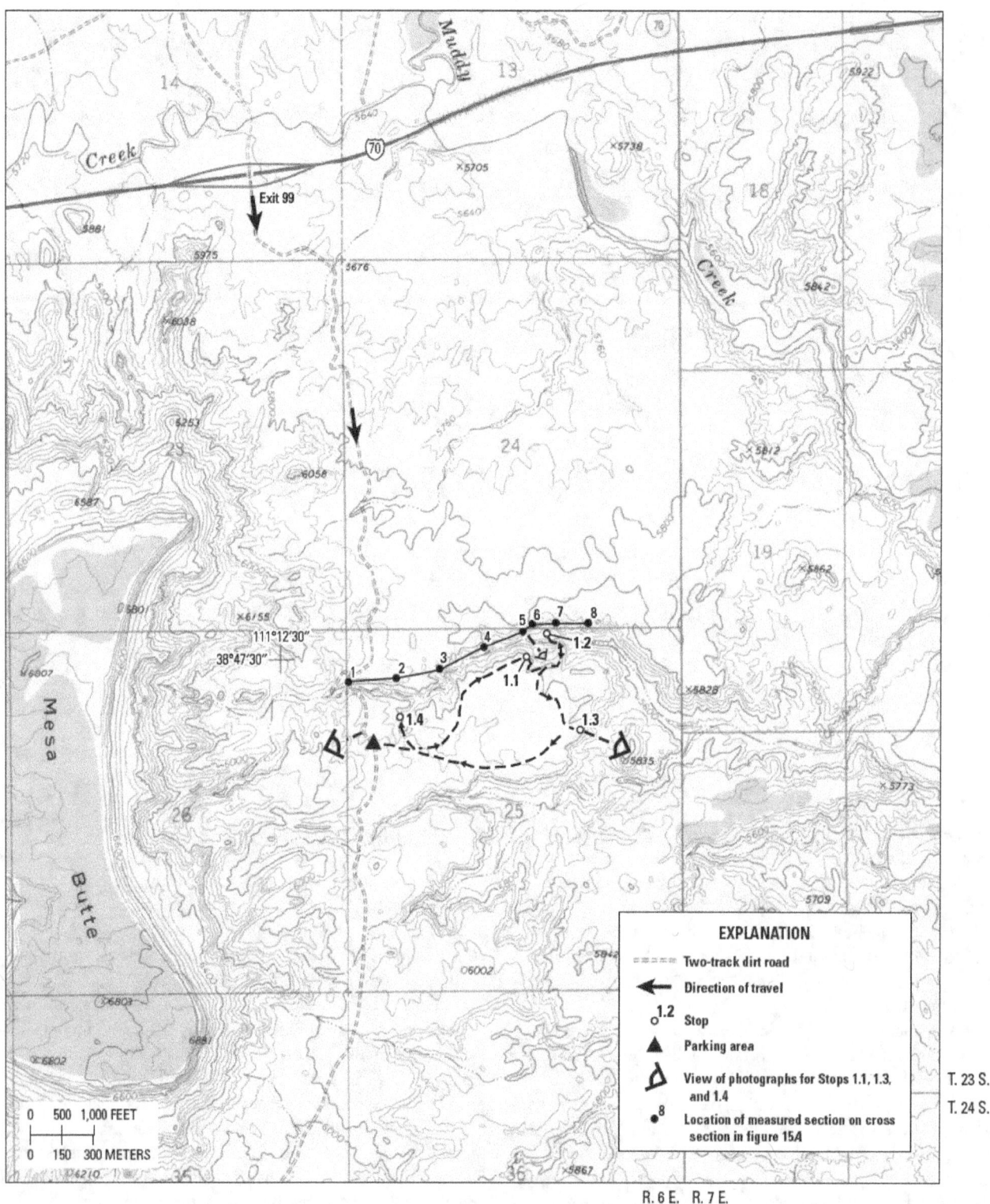

**Figure 14.**    Locations of Stops 1.1, 1.2, 1.3, and 1.4 as shown on part of the Mesa Butte 7.5-minute quadrangle. Exit from Interstate 70 at Exit 99 and proceed south on two-track dirt road (road is impassible when wet) to parking area.

An additional component for compartmentalization is the length of the channel (fig. 7). It is easy to foresee the drilling density that might be needed to access all of the potential compartments in an incised valley-fill deposit. The lengths of the sandstone bodies will be addressed at Stop 2, where one can walk out some of these sandstone bodies longitudinally, down depositional dip.

## Stop 1.2   Dinosaur Footprints

Stop 1.2 requires a steep descent into the drainage and part way up the other side of the drainage and then a return to Stop 1.1.

### Objectives

The stop is subsidiary to the main focus of the trip but is of interest to view dinosaur trackways in fallen blocks of the Dakota.

### Discussion

The tracks are exposed on the bottom of multiple blocks that have fallen away from the main Dakota outcrop (fig. 16). We believe these blocks are from the sandstone body near the top of the main amalgamated sandstone unit. The tracks are common in the area and indicate the stream bed may have been used for ease of movement through the landscape.

## Stop 1.3   Amalgamated Sandstone

After returning to the top of the southern rim of the side drainage, proceed southeast on an easy traverse for about 1,000 ft to the eastern edge of the Dakota outcrops (fig. 14). The stop is west of a conical hill shown in figure 14, and the photograph panel (fig. 17) was taken from that hill. The sandstone is best viewed from below and the best lighting for photographs is in the morning.

### Objectives

The point of this stop is to view a well-exposed depositional dip oriented outcrop of two of the sandstone bodies associated with the amalgamated sandstone facies. The main lithofacies seen here are the large-scale cross stratification with numerous reactivation surfaces (figs. 6 and 17).

### Discussion

Sand body 1, the lowest stratigraphically (fig. 17), is not as well exposed as sand body 2, but is unique to the study interval because of the amount of soft sediment deformation present at this locality. Soft sediment deformation is common, and it is apparent from relict sedimentary structures that much of this facies originally was large-scale cross stratification (fig. 17E). Another unique facies of the Dakota can be seen at this locality (fig. 17D). It has a basal irregular scour filled with massive disorganized sand that is apparently related to scour holes or pits eroded into the bottom of the channel by strong currents.

Sand body 2 has well-preserved, large-scale cross stratification with well-developed reactivation surfaces. Cross beds are relatively horizontal in the third dimension, indicating deposition from straight-crested, two-dimensional dunes. There also is large-scale trough cross stratification. Reactivation surfaces typically are associated with tidal or eolian deposits, but also are common in fluvial deposits (Collinson, 1970; McCabe and Jones, 1977). The large-scale stratification at this locality is present at the top of the sandstone body; cross stratification in the lower part consists of multiple thin beds (fig. 17C).

The large scale nature of the upper preserved bed, the generally unidirectional paleocurrent directions, and context with other sedimentary structures (fig. 15D) indicate a fluvial environment of deposition. The multiple reactivation surfaces indicate fluctuating flows. Poor preservation of the lowest sets is interpreted to indicate multiple periods of erosion within these channels and the development of barforms building within channels. The relatively small size of the sandstone bodies and lack of overbank deposits or wings to the sand bodies as seen at Stop 1.1 indicates a confined system for these channel bodies. We suggest the possibility that the large-scale cross stratification was formed from straight to slightly sinuous barforms that may have extended across most of the entire sand body modified by small channels and superimposed lunate dunes (see fig. 11A).

### Reservoir Considerations

This stop shows the level of complexity within the valley fill at a more detailed level by viewing two sand bodies oriented parallel to the paleoflow direction. The variation in thickness and continuity of the individual sedimentary structures should create considerable variations in permeability, and indicate the possibility of compartments within the sand body itself. Willis (1998) showed more variability between major valley bodies than within individual bodies, although he does document considerable variability within some fills. Even within the large-scale crossbeds seen at this locality there may be permeability variations (for comparison, see Willis and White, 2000, facies five, their fig. 4).

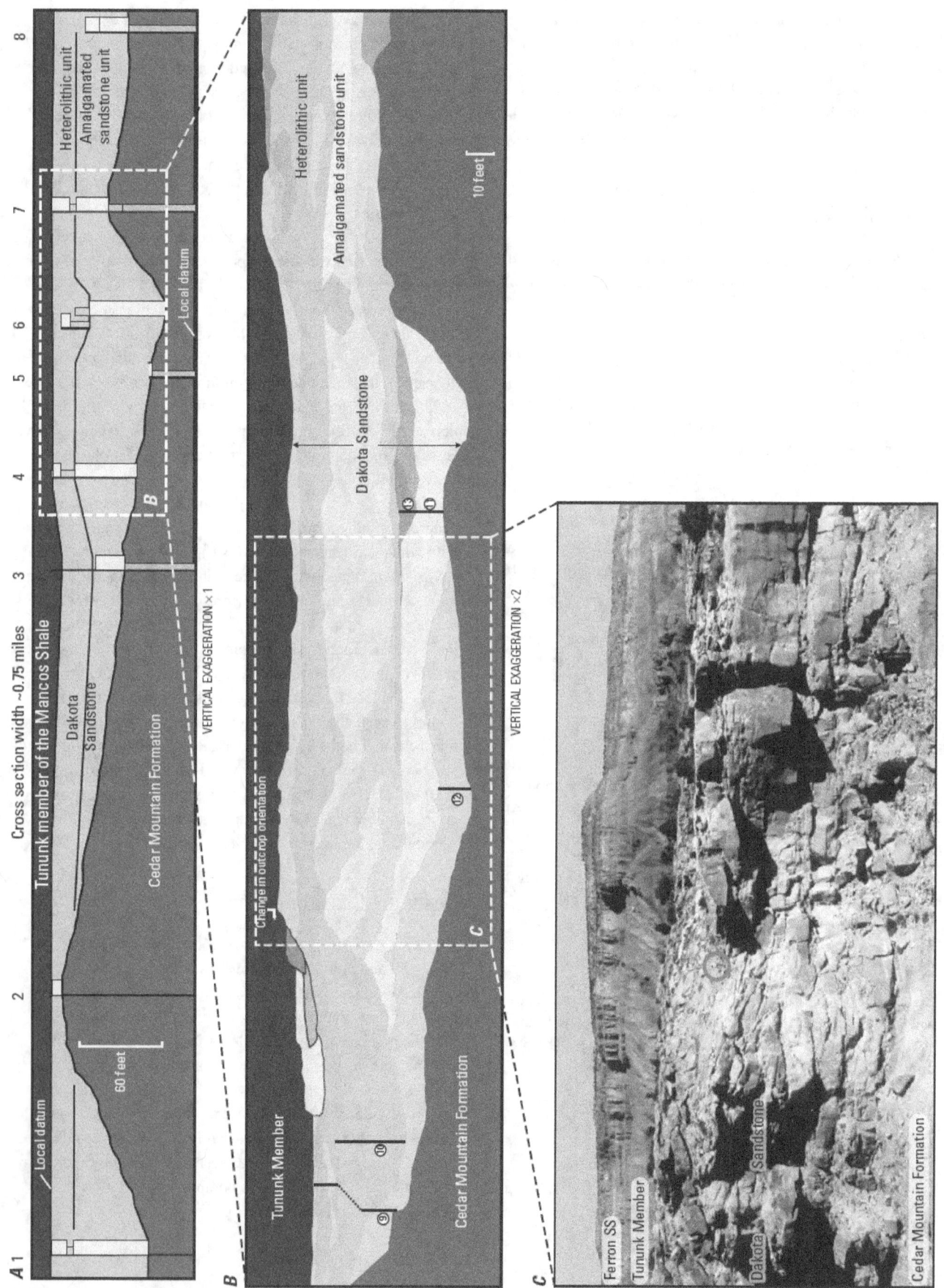

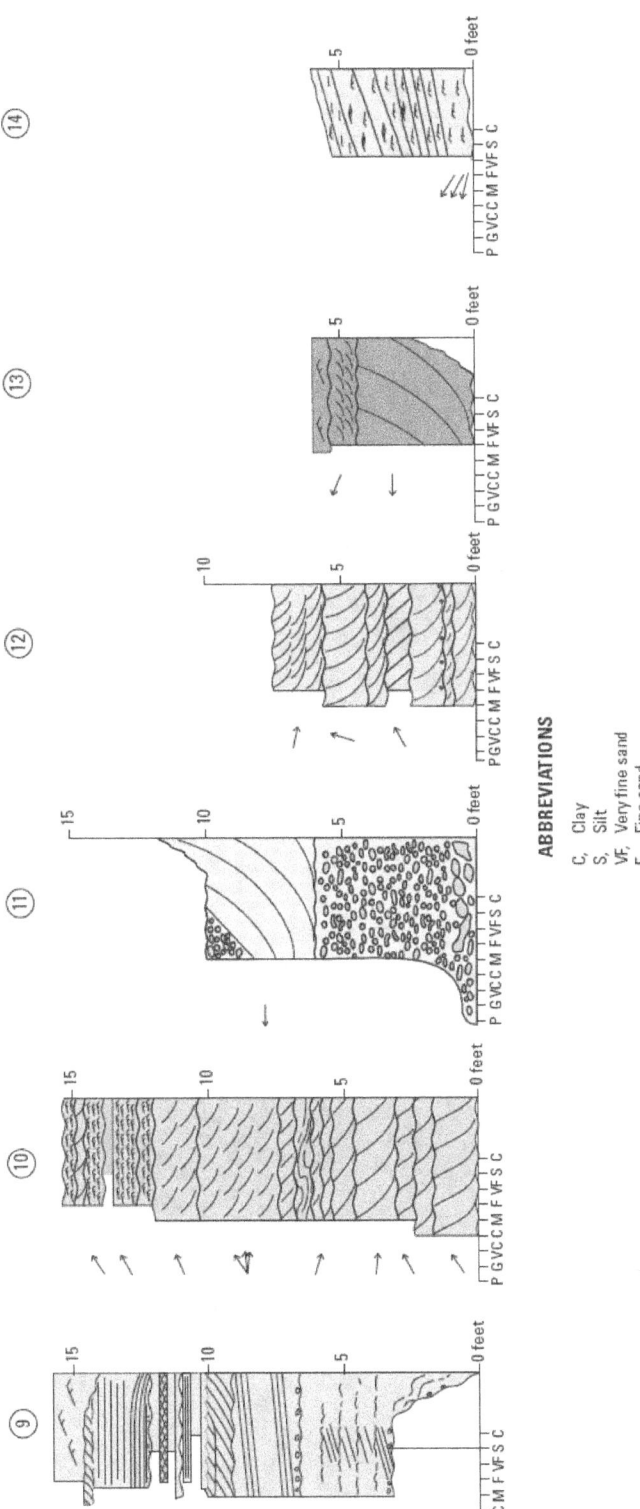

**ABBREVIATIONS**

C,    Clay
S,    Silt
VF,   Very fine sand
F,    Fine sand
M,    Medium sand
C,    Coarse sand
VC,   Very coarse sand
G,    Granules
P,    Pebbles

**Figure 15.**   (A) Stratigraphic cross section constructed across a depositional strike section in the main side canyon east of Mesa Butte (fig. 14) showing the general distribution of facies in the Cedar Mountain Formation, Dakota Sandstone, and Tununk Member of the Mancos Shale. At bottom, measured sections start from distinctive bed in the Cedar Mountain Formation. The section shows greater than 60 feet of incision of the Dakota into the underlying Cedar Mountain. Note how uncomplicated the valley fill looks from this generalized portrayal. (B) Diagram generalized from plate 1, showing an expanded view of part of panel A. Note change of direction of outcrop, which makes the left side of the diagram out of proportion with the right side—compare to plate 1. Diagram emphasizes the channel geometry, internal mudrock intervals in light gray and overall enclosure of sandstone within shale facies of the Tununk (black) and Cedar Mountain (dark gray). Locations of detailed measured sections are shown by numbers that correspond to sections on D. (C) Expanded view of part of panel B showing complexity of sandstone bodies in the Dakota. Person in blue circle is 5 feet in height. (D) Representative measured sections from channel bodies of the Dakota. All but measured section 14 are from the lower amalgamated facies and the numbers are keyed to figure 15B. Note the considerable variability between the sections in terms of sedimentary structures and thickness, but the general consistency in grain size.

**Figure 16.** (*A*) Single dinosaur footprint from the amalgamated sandstone facies of the Dakota Sandstone. Coin shown for scale. (*B*) Fallen block showing sandstone filling the top of older sandstone body with ripples and a distinct footprint trackway; location is from the lower right corner of *C*. (*C*) View of fallen blocks—mottled pattern indicates the presence of footprints. (*D*) Western part of Dakota exposure in main side canyon, with numerous fallen blocks that contain dinosaur tracks and showing the probable in-place location of blocks.

**Figure 17.** (*A*) Photomosaic of Dakota Sandstone outcrop at Stop 1.3 (fig. 14) taken from conical hill just to the east. Outcrop is oriented about N 30° E (person is 6 feet in height). (*B*) Line drawing of *A*; paleocurrents are shown by black arrows and are oriented with respect to the points of a compass. (*C*) Close-up view of sand body 2 located just to the left of where the person (circled) is standing in *A*; photograph courtesy of Steve Cumella, Bill Barrett Corporation; white arrows point to crossbed set boundaries; note that the sets increase in thickness upward. (*D*) Scour hole in sand body 1, a common structure in the Dakota, possibly caused by flow around an obstruction or by helical flow at the confluence of two channels (Ashmore and Parker, 1983). (*E*) Toesets of two large crossbeds overlain by convoluted bedding because of soft sediment deformation.

## Stop 1.4    Ribbon Sandstone Bodies

The next stop is back near the vehicles in the south half of the northwest quarter of section 25 (fig. 14). From Stop 1.3, it is a one-half mile easy traverse back to the west (fig. 14). A view of the locality is provided in figure 18A and it may be best to reorient oneself by returning to the road before proceeding to Stop 1.4. The best time for viewing these outcrops begins in the early afternoon and continues until the late afternoon.

### Objectives

At this stop, there are numerous ribbon sandstone bodies exposed in three dimensions, including exhumed sinuous sandstone bodies that can be walked out for hundreds of feet. The discussion at this stop invariably focuses on whether these sand bodies are channels or small deltas. Our conclusion is that they are channels of a low-gradient, relatively low-energy anastomosed channel system.

### Discussion

The sandstone bodies generally are 5- to 6-ft thick, but can be as thick as 12 ft, and are of short lateral extent, generally less than 50 ft, partly or totally enclosed within mudrock. The sandstones are fine to medium grained and predominantly ripple laminated. They have prominent accretion surfaces that dip as much as 27 degrees, although they range mostly between 14 to 25 degrees in their steepest parts based on about 15 measurements at this locality. Paleoflow is oblique and perpendicular to the accretion surfaces based on measurements obtained from ripples (fig. 18C). One sandstone body is about 30 ft wide and can be walked out in a slightly sinuous path for about 200 ft (fig. 18B). The sandstone bodies are interpreted to be channel deposits because of their overall fining upward grain size and upward decrease in flow strength. The lateral accretion surfaces and sinuous form of the channels indicate a meandering pattern; however, the narrow width of the channels indicates a narrow stream. These channels were short-lived and did not meander far across the floodplain.

The sandstone bodies overall are enclosed within finer grained organic-rich facies. The presence of minor coal, carbonaceous shale, and leaf fossils indicates some freshwater influence, but the presence of rare *Ophiomorpha* burrows, brackish water bivalves, and oysters also indicates local marine or tidal influence. Rare symmetrical ripples indicate local wave influence.

## Stop 2    Red Valley Area

Stop 2 is located about 2 mi due north of Mesa Butte, on the edge of an area called Red Valley (fig. 1, point RV). Drive back to I-70 from Stop 1, cross over it on the overpass, and continue straight ahead on the paved road up Muddy Creek toward Emery, Utah. At about 1 mi from the overpass (in the southwest quarter of section 12) there will be a two-track dirt road heading east across Muddy Creek, with public access through private property (fig. 19). The road bends to the south onto public land and it may be prudent to park in this area and walk before the road swings back to the east and down into a dry wash. Depending on the condition of the road, you can drive to within a few hundred feet of the stop. The traverse follows one sandstone to the north (sand body 1) and returns on parallel sandstone (sand body 2) back to the vehicles (see fig. 19). If you walk the road it is over one-half mile of moderate terrain and grade.

### Objectives

At this location, our position is closer to the western edge of the valley than at Stop 1 at Mesa Butte. From aerial and satellite photography there appear to be exhumed paleochannels at this locality. On the ground, these exposed channels do appear to be exhumed by erosion of the overlying marine shale of the Tunuck and undercut from erosion into the white bentonitic shale of the underlying Cedar Mountain Formation.

The primary purpose of the stop is to examine two sandstone complexes, one containing the higher energy cross-stratified facies and the other containing the ripple-bedded facies. The juxtaposition of the two facies in parallel sandstone complexes makes this location unique, and that they occupy the same apparent stratigraphic position based on the amount of erosion into the underlying bentonitic mudrock of the Cedar Mountain.

### Discussion

This area is of interest because of the apparent exhumed topography created by the weathering of the Tunuck Member exposing remnants of Dakota Sandstone. Sinuous sections of channel sandstone bodies appear to be preserved within enclosing shale, but another possibility is that the Dakota once covered the entire surface and now has been selectively eroded. Unfortunately, the entire outcrop is modified extensively by the erosion and undercutting of the Dakota sandstone bodies and it is difficult to reconstruct the true geometry of the bodies. In other areas where there is continuous Dakota, elements of sinuous sand bodies also can be identified (fig. 7). This traverse gives insight into the length of Dakota sand bodies, which are as long as 4,000 ft but only 100-ft wide (fig. 7).

## Stop 2.1    Channel Edge Sand Body 1

After driving or walking to the easternmost parking area, walk to the northeast towards the apparent bifurcation of the Dakota near Stop 2.1 (fig. 19). The termination of the sandstone outcrop is mainly made up of blocks of sandstone dropped by undercutting of the white-weathering bentonitic

**Figure 18.** (A) Overview of Stop 1.4 taken from the road at the parking area (figure 14 at parking area). (B) Typical sandstone of the upper facies of the Dakota Sandstone displaying well developed inclined surfaces dipping 12 to 15 degrees to the northeast (vertical rod colors are 1 foot increments). (C) Closer view of dipping bedding planes in the sandstone at B, and measured section (measured section 14 on figure 15D) showing that the sandstone is composed predominately of current ripple lamination. Note that the paleocurrent directions of the ripples (arrows) are about 90 degrees to the inclined bedding surfaces and these surfaces are interpreted as lateral accretion surfaces.

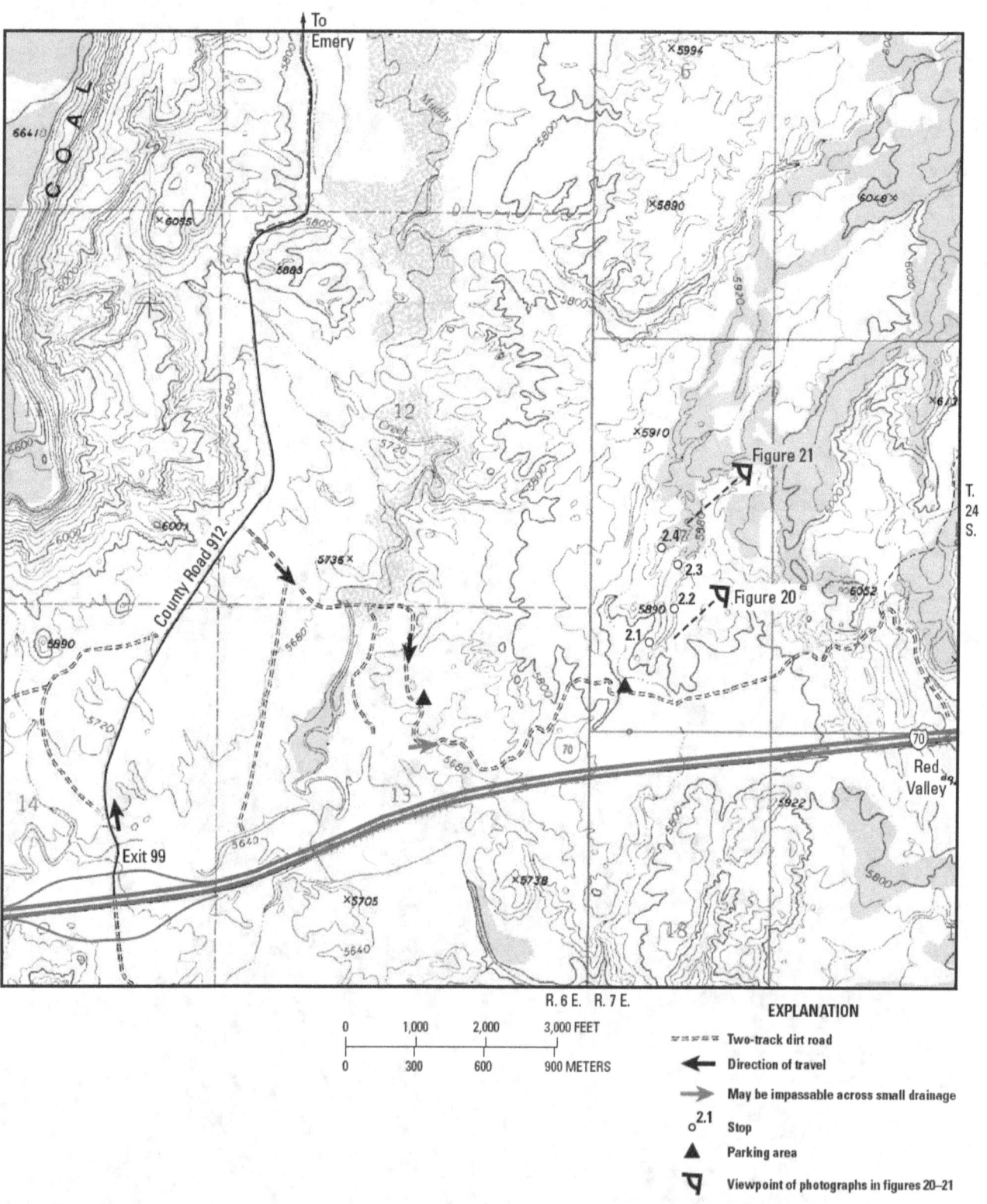

**Figure 19.**    Upper part of the Red Valley area just north of Interstate 70 and Stop 1 at Mesa Butte taken from the Mesa Butte 7.5-minute topographic quadrangle. The two separate parking areas reflect whether the road is passable across a small drainage marked by blue arrow below westernmost parking area.

mudrock of the underlying Cedar Mountain Formation. The stop is at the first inplace outcrop on the west side of the exposure (fig. 20A), where the sandstone displays three bedsets in about 15 ft of section (fig. 20B). The lowest bed displays climbing ripples with a relatively high angle of climb but still without stoss side preservation indicating high sedimentation rates. The middle bed is cross stratified with multiple reactivation surfaces and some topset preservation; it is trough shaped in the third dimension, indicating episodic fluctuating flows of three-dimensional dunes moving as discrete bedforms. The upper bed contains abundant ripup clasts, cross beds, and convoluted beds all indicative of a channel fill. The scale and flow velocity of the units are indicative of the fluvial amalgamated sandstone facies of the Dakota. Note that the general transport direction is north-northeast.

## Stop 2.2    Traverse of Top Surface of Sand Body 1

Climb to the top of the sand body 1 and walk along the top toward the northeast. Note that many of the blocks are highly unstable. Hike to the point where the next apparent bifurcation joins this body from the west. Photograph figure 20A shows a view back to Stop 2.1 and also shows the general location of Stop 1 where one can observe a definite transition from the amalgamated sandstone facies into the heterolithic facies to the west. The view back to the north shows continuous sandstone to the northeast, whereas the sandstone is much more irregularly preserved to the northwest. Note that the sandstone body appears to cut, and therefore is younger than, the next adjoining channel at Stop 2.2. At several points along the traverse you can descend over the edge to observe the facies. Photographs in figures 20C and 20D show beds with the same type of cross stratification as seen elsewhere. These are overlain by beds with horizontal to slightly dipping bedding that up close are seen to be low-angle preservation ripples (pseudo-horizontal lamination) indicative of superimposed ripples moving in shallow water and erosively removing the stoss side of the older ripple form.

## Stops 2.3 and 2.4    View and Traverse of Sand Body 2

Continue on to the northeast to Stop 2.3 (fig. 19). One should now be able to see another sandstone body to the west (fig. 21A), trending parallel to the body just walked on for about 1,000 ft, the entire length of the body is about 1,800 ft before it is separated by undercutting. However, it appears to continue further based on satellite views and the trend of the body. As an aside, note the strong joint pattern in the Dakota Sandstone that parallels the trend of the west limb of the San Rafael Swell (also seen in fig. 21B). The Dakota is broken up badly by undercutting of the jointed blocks; therefore, one needs to climb down to the west to avoid jumbled blocks of sandstone that make walking difficult.

Sand body 2 (fig. 21) is disconnected from the previous sandstone, and it is unclear how or if the two are connected. Sand body 2 actually is a complex of multiple bedsets and the main observation is in the uppermost part of the complex, where cross stratification clearly shows transport to the southwest, which is 180 degrees to the transport direction of sand body 1. When one walks over to Stop 2.4, the bedsets show a variety of sedimentary structures, but they are mainly subcritical- to supercritical climbing ripples (fig. 21C, E). The sand body contains rare burrows including probable escape structures (fig. 21D) and straight, vertical, sand-filled tubes resembling Skolithos.

The southerly paleocurrent directions, low-energy fill, ripples, and rare burrows are interpreted to be related to the uppermost heterolithic facies. The sandstone is probably an entirely younger fill than sand body 1 even though the sand bodies occupy the same stratigraphic position. No part of this sandstone is likely related to the oldest part of the fill at Mesa Butte.

## Reservoir Considerations

This stop allows one to walk along the length of, and within, two sandstone bodies located at the margins of the valley complex in order to obtain a three-dimensional view of a reservoir compartment. Within this part of the valley fill the sandstone body compartments are enclosed with mudrock, so fluid flow would be directed along the length of the body. It is not clear to what degree there would be transmission of fluids between bodies where they are superimposed in the main part of the valley fill.

## Stop 3    Caineville Reef Area Interfluvial Area Between Valley Systems

The stop is between Hanksville and Torrey, Utah along State Highway 24 (fig. 22). From Stop 2, the Caineville area can be accessed by two different routes: however, the most scenic is through Capitol Reef National Monument, a distance of about 90 miles and requiring about 2 hours driving time.

Return to I-70 from Stop 2 and head west on I-70. Take Exit 91 and head south under the overpass and take an immediate right turn (west) to access State Highway 72 heading to Fremont and Loa, Utah (fig. 13). After traveling about 30 mi and passing through Fremont, Utah, State Highway 72 terminates at State Highway 24. Turn left (east) and drive for about 40 mi passing through Lyman, Bicknell, Torrey, and Capitol Reef National Monument. It is easy to get distracted in Capitol Reef and field trips usually make a couple of brief stops for both scenic and geologic interest.

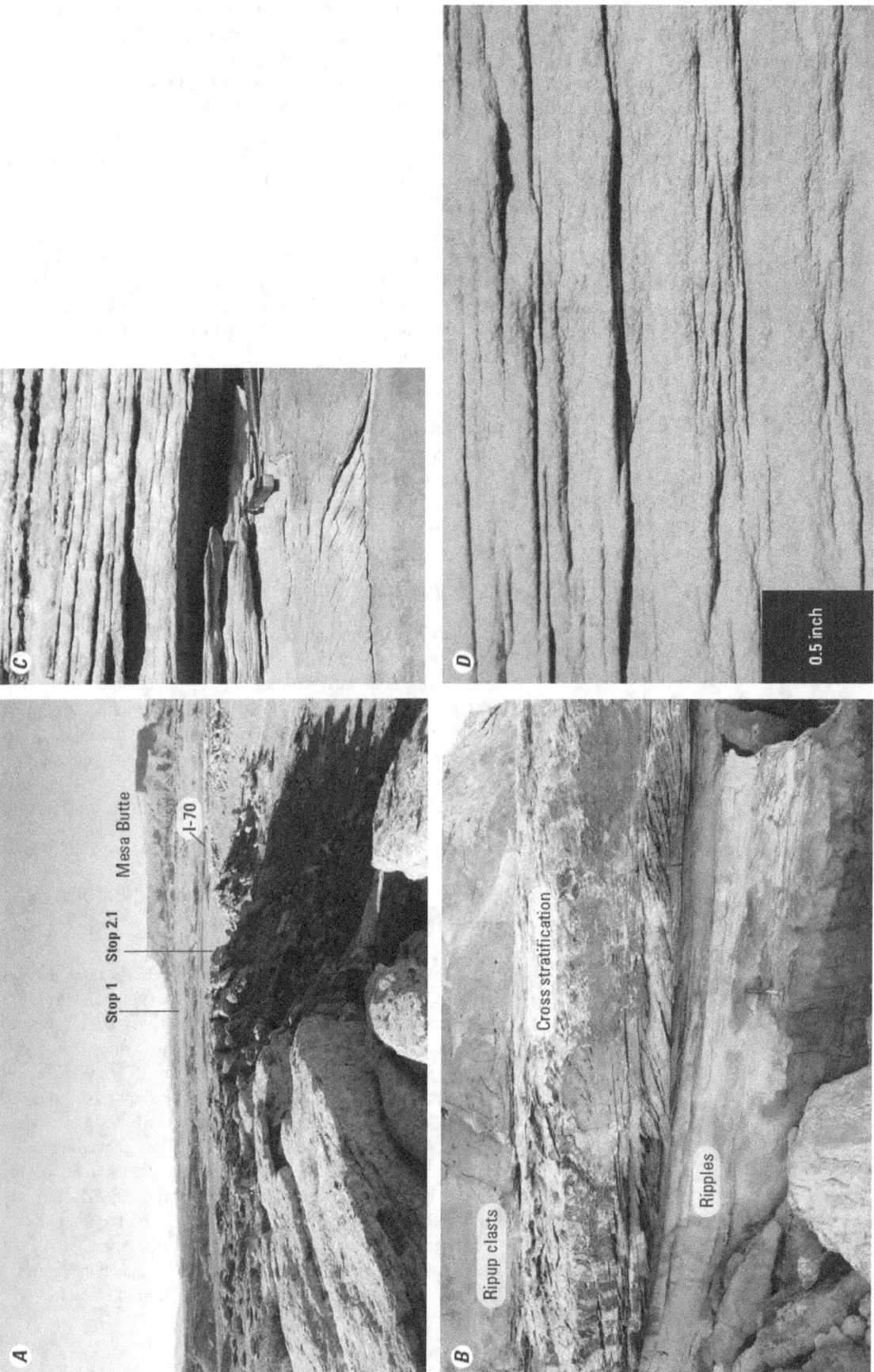

**Figure 20.** (A) Overview of general area of Stop 2; photograph taken from Stop 2.2 looking to the southwest toward Stop 1, Mesa Butte, and Stop 2.1. (B) Stop 2.1, located at the edge of the exhumed sinuous multistory sandstone body (sand body 1) visible on figure 19. From the parking area, it is the nearest exposure that is fully in place. The lowest bed consists of climbing ripples, barely visible in the photograph, and the middle bed displays small- to medium-scale cross stratification with reactivation surfaces and partial topset preservation. Out of view to the right can be seen the third dimension of the forms and small- to medium-scale trough forms that indicate deposition as three-dimensional dunes. The upper bed contains numerous ripup clasts at its base indicating a separate channel body from the lower bed. (C) Bedding at east of edge of sandstone body at Stop 2.2, including small-scale cross stratification in the lower part and slightly inclined beds in the upper part of C, consisting of subcritically climbing ripples with little preservation, giving rise to pseudo-horizontal lamination. (D) Detail of lamination in the upper part of C, consisting of subcritically climbing ripples with little preservation, giving rise to pseudo-horizontal lamination.

**Figure 21.**  (*A*) Sand body 2 of the Dakota Sandstone at Stop 2.4 as viewed from the northeast from Stop 2.3 showing the location of photographs at *B*, *C* and *E*. (*B*) View from south of Stop 3 showing part of sandstone at Stop 4; note the cross stratification at the top of the sandstone at the left side of the photograph that are clearly indicating paleocurrent direction is to the left, which is 180 degrees opposite to the sandstone we are now standing on. (*C*) Close-up view of the northeastern part of the sandstone body (see *A* for location) consisting of supercritical to subcritical climbing ripple strata. (*D*) Large trace fossil in upper part of sandstone body. (*E*) Even bedding composed of subcritical ripple strata typical of the upper facies of the Dakota.

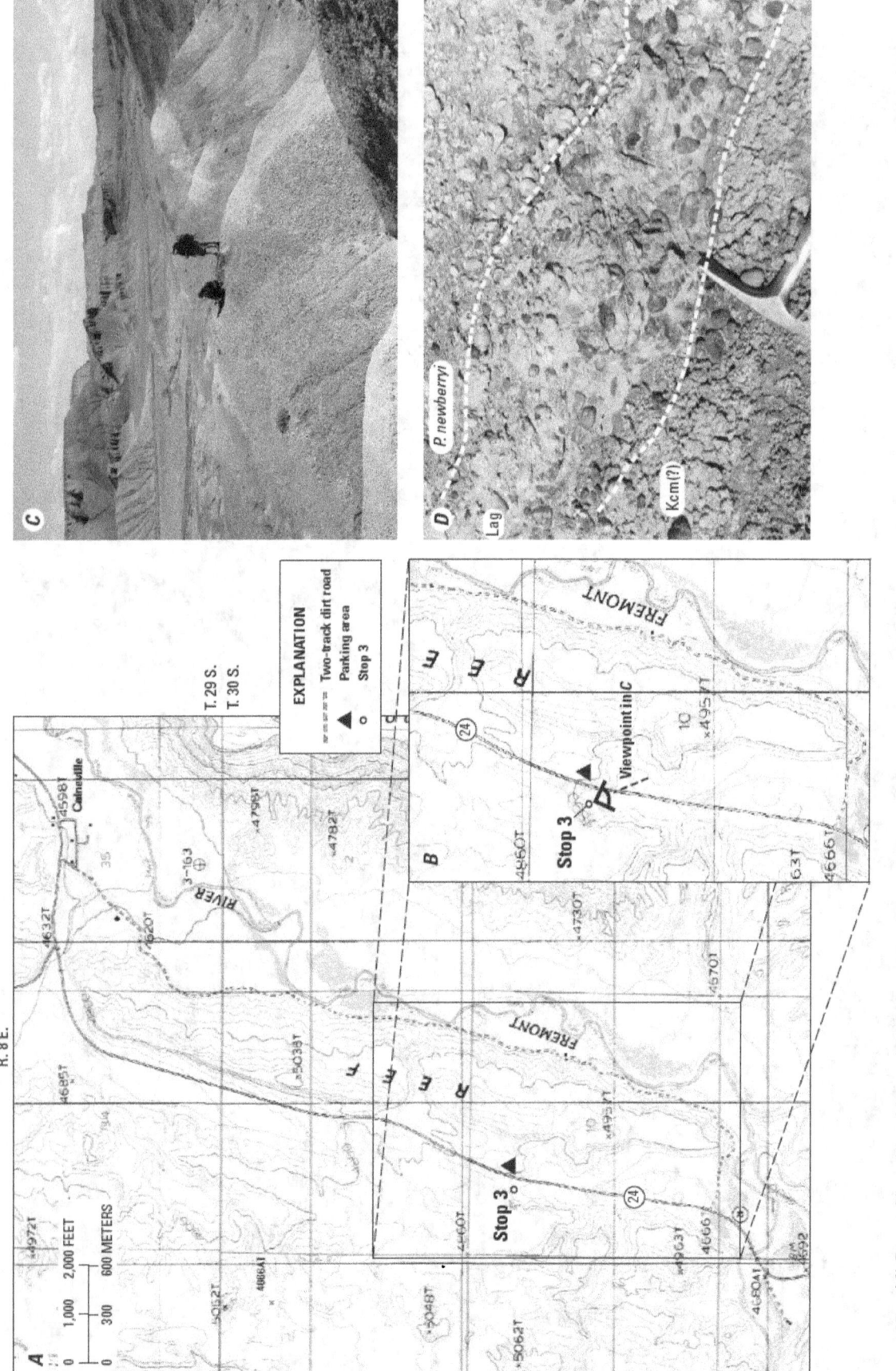

**Figure 22.**    (*A*) General location of Stop 3 in relation to Caineville, Utah and the intersection of the Fremont River and State Highway 24. (*B*) Inset shows location of Stop 3 and parking area in road cut of Tununk Member of the Mancos Shale. (*C*) View looking southeast towards State Highway 24. Note the purple-gray mudrock beds of the underlying Cedar Mountain Formation (?) in right middle ground (photograph courtesy of Steve Cumella, Bill Barrett Corporation). (*D*) Mudstone, overlain by a pebble lag, which is all that remains of the Dakota, overlain by the *Pycnodonte newberryi* oyster deposit of the basal Tununk Member (photograph courtesy of Jeff May, EOG Resources).

The road follows the Fremont River through Capitol Reef (fig. 13), passes out of the park, and crosses the river, which moves out of view to the east of the Ferron Sandstone Member of the Mancos Shale (fig. 3). After crossing the river, the road straightens and flattens out for about one-half mile and begins to rise topographically. Park at the road cut exposing the Tununk Member of the Mancos Shale, in the north end of section 10 (fig. 22). Walk back down the road toward Capitol Reef and traverse to the west to the contact between the Tununk Member and the Cedar Mountain(?)/ Morrison Formation.

Alternately, if driving from the east side of the San Rafael Swell, from Hanksville drive west on Highway 24 to Caineville, a distance of about 18 miles. Continue west on Highway 24 (pass through dipping Ferron Sandstone Member) the road bends to the south and heads up a rise. At about 1.5 mi from Caineville you pass through a road cut of the Tununk Member. Park at the road cut. Proceed to the south on foot, down the road until you can head west on relatively level ground to the base of the Tununk Shale (see map fig. 22B).

## Objectives

The significance of this stop is not what one can see, but what one cannot see. There is no Dakota Sandstone. One can see: (1) a carbonate-nodule-bearing mudrock unit that is either part of the Cedar Mountain Formation or Morrison Formation, (2) a chert-pebble lag that represents the remnant of the Dakota, (3) an oyster deposit consisting exclusively of Pycnodonte newberryi (fig. 22D), and (4) marine mudrock of the Tununk Member of the Mancos Shale.

## Discussion

At this locality, there are no deposits of the Dakota Sandstone. This area is interpreted to be an interfluvial area between two valley complexes that trend to the north-northeast: one on the west side of the Swell, seen at Mesa Butte and Red Valley, and one in the southern part of the Swell near the Henry Mountains. For other Dakota rocks in the Henry Mountains area, see Hunt and others (1953, their figure 19). This interfluve matches up with the lack of Dakota on the east side of the San Rafael Swell. The conglomerate and pebbly sandstone observed on the eastern part of the Swell are interpreted to be the basal beds of the Mussentuchits member of the Cedar Mountain Formation.

At Stop 3, the basal Dakota unconformity and transgressive marine surface of the Dakota merge and the resulting hiatus represents at least 2 m.y. of time (fig. 3). One would expect a major paleosol to be present at this location, but if it was ever present it may have been eroded by wave ravinement during marine transgression as represented by the chert-pebble lag. To the north, just before Caineville, there is a dirt road that heads off to the north (at the base of the Ferron Sandstone Member) that heads up to another outcrop of the Dakota.

At these northern locations, there is carbonaceous shale and thin coal occupying the space between the two unconformities. The coal probably represents the record of the paleosol that developed during rising freshwater tables on the coastal plain associated with transgression of the overlying Tununk Member (figs. 3 and 5).

## Reservoir Considerations

The interfluvial area bounds the valley and demonstrates the existence of lateral seals for the valley-fill deposit.

## Stop 4    Blue Valley—Back in Another Valley-Fill Complex

From Stop 3, go eastbound on State Highway 24 through Caineville for approximately 13.5 mi. At about 9 mi you will reach the top of a mesa held up by the Ferron Sandstone Member of the Mancos Shale, and Factory Butte will be visible to the left (north). Proceed down section through the Ferron and out onto a flat stretch of road. The road crosses a small drainage flowing into the Fremont River, and one can see the view in figure 23B located in the extreme uppermost center of section 22 (fig. 23) Turn left and park along the dirt road coming in from the north through section 15.

If driving from Hanksville, the parking area is about 6.5 miles west of the junction of State Highway 24 with State Highway 95. This location also is described in an excellent field guide by Fielding and others (2010).

## Objectives

The Dakota Sandstone at this location consists of three variations of the facies that were seen at Mesa Butte: (1) a conglomeratic and cross bedded pebbly sandstone facies (fig. 24B), (2) a heterolithic facies dominated by burrowed, inclined heterolithic strata (figs. 24C, D), and (3) a burrowed sandstone facies with pebbles and oyster fossils (fig. 24E, F). The unit is overlain by Tununk Member containing the same late Cenomanian oyster (P. newberryi) as at Mesa Butte.

## Discussion

The Dakota Sandstone at this location rests unconformably on the Cedar Mountain Formation (Lawyer, 1972; Fielding and others, 2010) or the Morrison Formation (fig. 24A, E) (Young, 1960), depending on the interpretation. The underlying unit here is a mottled variegated mudrock that is interpreted as a paleosol (B. Currie, Miami University, oral commun., 1998). The Dakota is overlain by the Tununk Member containing Pycnodonte newberryi, a late Cenomanian marine oyster that is also present on the San Rafael Swell. The age of the Dakota at this locality is not constrained other than by the age of the oyster; however, the stratigraphic position

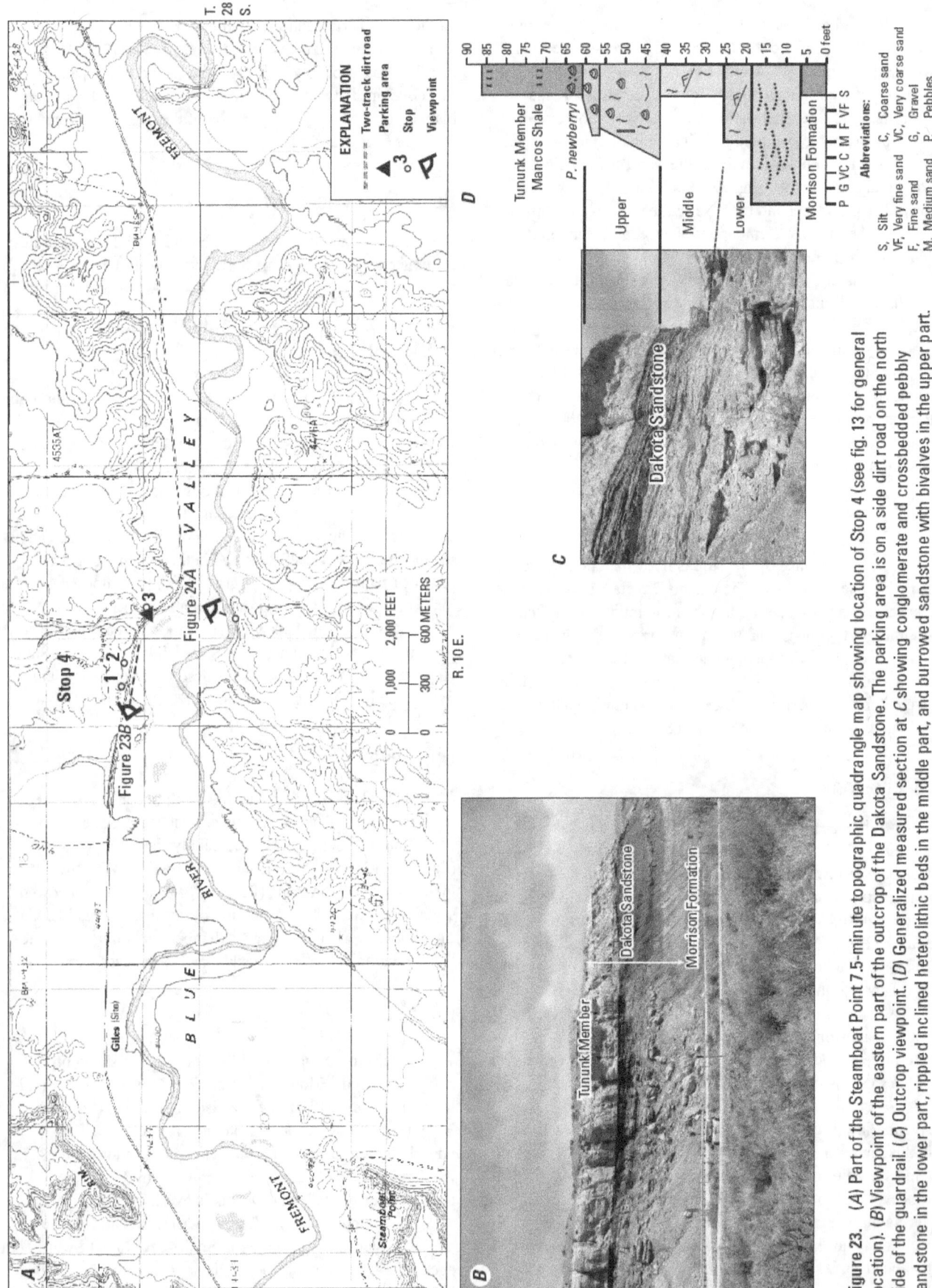

**Figure 23.** (A) Part of the Steamboat Point 7.5-minute topographic quadrangle map showing location of Stop 4 (see fig. 13 for general location). (B) Viewpoint of the eastern part of the outcrop of the Dakota Sandstone. The parking area is on a side dirt road on the north side of the guardrail. (C) Outcrop viewpoint. (D) Generalized measured section at C showing conglomerate and crossbedded pebbly sandstone in the lower part, rippled inclined heterolithic beds in the middle part, and burrowed sandstone with bivalves in the upper part.

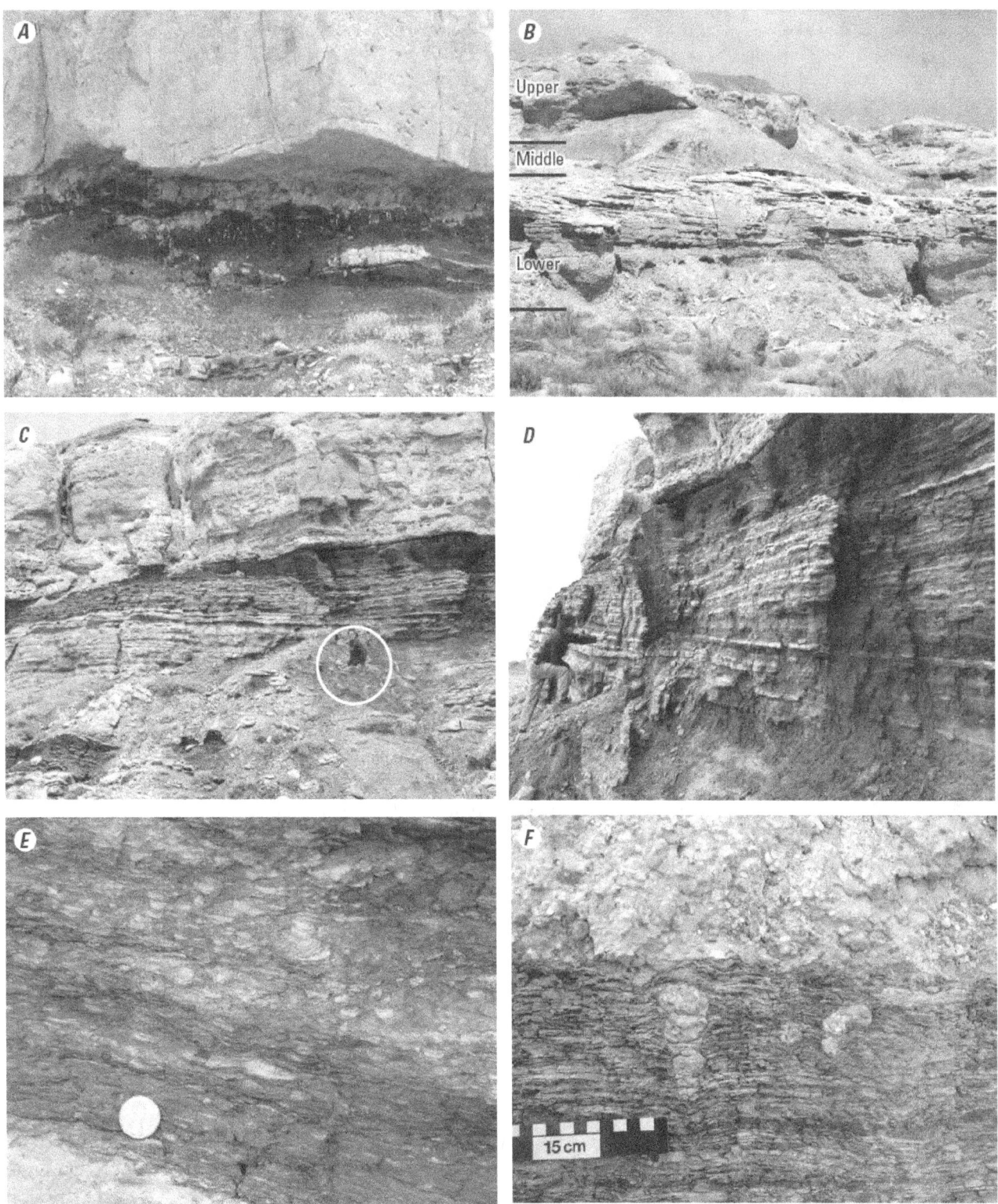

**Figure 24.**    (*A*) View of contact between variegated mudrock of the Morrison Formation and the sandstone of the Dakota (location on fig. 23*A*). (*B*) View of outcrops north of Stop 4.3. Outcrops showing the 3 parts of the Dakota Sandstone about 50 feet thick—upper, middle, and lower. This locality is the best place to see the conglomerate and pebbly cross bedded sandstone facies of the lower part of the Dakota. Note the large-scale bedding that dips left to right across the lower sandstone. (*C*) Closer view of outcrop on fig. 23*B* showing heterolithic facies and upper burrowed sandstone facies; person circled for scale. (*D*) Closer view of inclined bedding in *C* with thin discontinuous sandstones and less resistant sandy mudrock. (*E*) Closer view of sandy mudrock with well preserved *Teichichnus* burrows. (*F*) Close-up view of contact between the heterolithic facies and the burrowed sandstone facies. Vertical to sub-vertical burrows filled with sand and chert granules of the upper unit of the Dakota.

indicates it is probably time equivalent to some part of the Dakota at Mesa Butte, but it could be as old as the Mussentuchit member of the Cedar Mountain Formation. The main purpose of this stop is to see the lateral variation in facies between here and Caineville Reef.

The section at Stop 4 was first measured by Hunt and others (1953) as part of a regional study of the Henry Mountains Basin and was later studied by Lawyer (1972) and Fielding and others (2010). All workers show the three part division of a lower conglomerate and pebbly sandstone, a middle organic-rich zone, and an upper burrowed shell-rich unit. The Dakota is 0 to 76 ft thick in the Henry Mountains Basin (Hunt and others, 1953).

The conglomerate and cross bedded pebbly sandstone are of probable fluvial origin, with paleocurrents oriented to the east-northeast (Lawyer, 1972). The conglomerate is reported to contain fossil wood (Lawyer, 1972). Large-scale cross stratification is interpreted as barforms built above a conglomeratic channel fill. The top has vertical, straight sand-filled (carbonaceous lined) traces that could be root traces or *Skolithos* (?) burrows.

The inclined heterolithic strata consist of thin discontinuous sandstone beds and interbedded mudrock with abundant carbonaceous material capped in most places by a thin coal bed. The sandstones are burrowed by abundant *Teichichnus* (fig. 24E), but where bedding is preserved it is streaky to wavy. These rocks fill a scour cut into the underlying sandstone facies (fig. 23B) and are interpreted to be the point bars of a tidal channel. The highly burrowed fill indicates slow deposition and reworking by monospecific burrowing possibly indicating fluctuating brackish and frequent freshwater influence. Brackish-water intrusion during low freshwater conditions would have possibly brought in larva of the organisms, which then died out during freshwater influx either by storms or seasonally. The fining upward grain size and decreasing upward energy levels within the main section along Highway 24 (fig. 23) indicates a gradual abandonment of

the channel and in filling with vegetation, including trees, as indicated by the thin coal at the top. Lawyer (1972) described a much more diverse trace fossil assemblage, but it is difficult to compare the traces with his described facies. This location shows much more estuarine influence than seen at Mesa Butte or Red Valley.

The upper sandstone unit has abundant oysters and rare pectins (Lawyer, 1972), indicating marine influence. Lawyer (1972) also noted some preserved symmetrical ripples indicating wave action, but the majority of the sandstone was reworked by burrowing. The most likely depositional environment is either shoreface or washover/flood-tidal-delta complex reworked into the upper part of the incised valley prior to marine flooding, wave ravinement, and deposition of marine shale.

## Reservoir Considerations

This locality is different to that observed at other localities with fluvial deposits because these fluvial facies are coarser grained and have the potential to have better porosity, although there is more mudrock overall in the upper part of the succession creating baffles to the reservoirs.

## Acknowledgments

We appreciate discussions with Mike Boyles, Steve Cumella, Brian Currie, Russ Dubiel, Jeff May, and Pete McCabe. Thanks to Dave Anderson for use of his paleocurrent program to calculate vector means in figure 1C, and to Wayne Husband, ATA Services, for drafting assistance and design of the cover. Selected photographs courtesy of Steve Cumella and Jeff May. Reviews by Russ Dubiel and Dick Keefer improved the report significantly. Doug Nichols reviewed the accuracy of stratigraphic names.

# References Cited

Ashmore, Peter, and Parker, Gary, 1983, Confluence scour in coarse braided streams: Water Resources Research, v. 19, no. 2, p. 392–402.

Cifelli, R.L., Kirkland, J.I., Weil, Anne, Deino, A.L., and Kowallis, B.J., 1997, High-precision 40Ar/39Ar geochronology and the advent of North America's Late Cretaceous terrestrial fauna: Proceedings of the National Academy of Science v. 94, p. 11163–11167.

Cobban, W.A., 1976, Ammonite record from the Mancos Shale of the Castle Valley-Price-Woodside area, east-central Utah: Brigham Young University Geology Series, v. 22, p. 117–126.

Cobban, W.A., Merewether, E.A., Fouch, T.D., and Obradovich, J.D., 1994, Some Cretaceous shorelines in the Western Interior of the United States, in Caputo, M.V., Peterson, J.A., and Franczyk, K.J., eds., Mesozoic Systems of the Rocky Mountain Region, USA: Rocky Mountain Section, Society of Economic Paleontologists and Mineralogists, p. 393–413.

Cobban, W.A., Walaszczyk, Ireneusz, Odradovich, J.D., and McKinney, K.C., 2006, A USGS zonal table for the Upper Cretaceous middle Cenomanian-Maastrichtian of the Western Interior of the United States based on Ammonites, Inoceramids, and radiometric ages: U.S. Geological Survey Open-File Report 2006–1250, 46 p.

Collinson, J.D., 1970, Bedforms of the Tana River, Norway: Geografiska Annaler, v. 52A, p. 31–56.

Cushman, R.A., 1994, Palynostratigraphy of the Upper Cretaceous Mancos Shale in western Colorado: Colorado School of Mines, Ph.D. dissertation, T-3466, 686 p.

Dalrymple, R.W., Boyd, Ron, and Zaitlin, B.A., editors, 1994, Incised-valley systems—Origin and sedimentary sequences: Society of Economic Petrologists and Mineralologists Special Publication 51, 391 p.

DeCelles, P.G., 2004, Late Jurassic to Eocene evolution of the Cordilleran thrust belt and foreland basin system, western U.S.A.: American Journal of Science, v. 304, p. 105–168.

Dolson, John, Muller, Dave, Evetts, M.J., and Stein, J.A., 1991, Regional paleotopographic trends and production, Muddy Sandstone (lower Cretaceous), central and northern Rocky Mountains: American Association of Petroleum Geologists Bulletin, v. 75, p. 409–435.

Eaton, J.G., Kirkland, J.I., and Kauffman, E.G., 1990, Evidence and dating of Mid-Cretaceous tectonic activity in the San Rafael Swell, Emery County, Utah: The Mountain Geologist, v. 27, no. 2, p. 39–45.

Fielding, C.R., Antia, Jonathan, Birgenheier, L.P., and Corbett, M.J., 2010, A field guide to the Cretaceous succession of the western Henry Mountains syncline, south-central Utah in Carney, S.M., Tabet, D.E., and Johnson, C.L. eds., Geology of south-central Utah: Utah Geological Association Publications 39, 41 p.

Garrison, J.R., Jr. Brinkman, Donald, Nichols, D.J., Layer, Paul, Burge, Donald, and Thayn, Denise, 2007, A multidisciplinary study of the Lower Cretaceous Cedar Mountain Formation, Mussentuchit Wash, Utah—A determination of the paleoenvironment and paleoecology of the *Eolambia caroljonesa* dinosaur quarry: Cretaceous Research, v. 28, p. 461–494.

Gilluly, James, 1929, Geology and oil and gas prospects of part of the San Rafael Swell Utah: U.S. Geological Survey Bulletin 806-C, p. 69–130.

Haq, B.U., Hardenbol, J., and Vail, P.R., 1987, Chronology of fluctuating sea levels since the Triassic: Science, v. 235, p. 1156–1167.

Henry, M.E., and Finn, T.M., 2003, Evaluation of undiscovered natural gas in the Upper Cretaceous Ferron Coal/Wasatch Plateau Total Petroleum System, Wasatch Plateau and Castle Valley, Utah in Collett, T.S. and Barker, C.E., eds., Coalbed methane in the Ferron Coals, Utah—A multidisciplinary study: International Journal of Coal Geology, v. 56 , p. 3–37.

Hunt, C.B., Averitt, Paul, and Miller, R.L., 1953, Geology and geography of the Henry Mountains region Utah: U.S. Geological Survey Professional Paper 228, 234 p.

Kauffman, E.G., and Pratt, L.M., 1985, A field guide to the stratigraphy, geochemistry, and depositional environments of the Kiowa-Skull Creek, Greenhorn, and Niobrara marine cycles in the Pueblo-Canon City area, Colorado, in Pratt, L.M., Kauffman, E.G., and Zelt, F.B., eds., Fine-grained deposits and biofacies of the Cretaceous Western Interior Seaway—Evidence of cyclic sedimentary processes: Society of Economic Paleontologists and Mineralogists Second Annual Midyear Meeting Field Trip Guidebook 4, p. Frs-1–Frs-26.

Kindinger, J.L., Balson, P.S., and Flocks, J.G., 1994, Stratigraphy of the Mississippi-Alabama shelf and the Mobile River incised valley system in Dalrymple, R.W., Boyd, Ron, and Zaitlin, B.A., eds., Incised-valley systems—Origin and sedimentary sequences: Society of Economic Petrologists and Mineralogists Special Publication 51, p. 81–95.

Kirkland, J.I., Britt, Brooks, Burge, D.L., Carpenter, Ken, Cifelli, Richard, Decourten, Frank, Eaton, Jeffery, Hasiotis, Steve, and Lawton, Tim, 1997, Lower to Middle Cretaceous dinosaur faunas of the central Colorado Plateau—A key to understanding 35 million years of tectonics, sedimentology, evolution and biogeography: Brigham Young University Geology Studies, v. 42, Part II, p. 69–103.

Kirschbaum, M.A., and McCabe, P.J., 1992, Controls on the accumulation of coal and on the development of anastomosed fluvial systems in the Cretaceous Dakota Formation of southern Utah: Sedimentology, v. 39, p. 581–599.

Kirschbaum, M.A., and Hettinger, R.D., 2004, Facies analysis and sequence stratigraphic framework of upper Campanian strata (Neslen and Mount Garfield Formations, Bluecastle Tongue of the Castlegate Sandstone, and Mancos Shale), eastern Book Cliffs, Colorado and Utah: U.S. Geological Survey Digital Data Series DDS 69-G, 40 p.

Lawton, T.F., 1985, Style and timing of frontal structures, thrust belt, central Utah: American Association of Petroleum Geologists Bulletin, v. 69, p. 1145–1159.

Lawyer, G.F., 1972, Sedimentary features and paleoenvironment of the Dakota Sandstone (early Upper Cretaceous) near Hanksville, Utah: Brigham Young University Geology Studies, v. 19, pt. 2, p. 89–120.

McCabe, P.J., and Jones, C.M., 1977, Formation of reactivation surfaces within superimposed deltas and bedforms: Journal of Sedimentary Geology, v. 47, no. 2, p. 707–715.

Obradovich, J.D., 1993, A Cretaceous time scale, *in* Caldwell, W.G.E., and Kauffman, E.G., eds., Evolution of the Western Interior Basin: Geological Association of Canada Special Paper 39, p. 379–396.

Picard, M.D., and Andersen, D.W., 1975, Paleocurrent analysis and orientation of sandstone bodies in the Duchesne River Formation (Eocene-Oligocene?), northern Uinta basin, northeastern Utah: Utah Geology, v. 2, n. 1, p. 1–15.

Pranter, M.A., Ellison, A.I., Cole, R.D., and Patterson, P.E., 2007, Analysis and modeling of intermediate-scale reservoir heterogeneity based on a fluvial point-bar outcrop analog, Williams Fork Formation, Piceance Basin, Colorado: American Association of Petroleum Geologists, v. 91, no. 7, p. 1025–1051.

Roberts, L.N.R., and Kirschbaum, M.A., 1995, Paleogeography of the Upper Cretaceous of the Western Interior of middle North America—Coal distribution and sediment accumulation: U.S. Geological Survey Professional Paper 1561, 116 p., 24 figs.

Sharp, J.V.A., 1963, Unconformities within basal marine Cretaceous rocks of the Piceance Basin, Colorado: University of Colorado, Ph.D. dissertation, 170 p.

Stokes, W.L., 1944, Morrison Formation and related deposits in and adjacent to the Colorado Plateau: Geological Society of America Bulletin, v. 55, no. 8, p. 951–992.

Stokes, W.L., 1952, Lower Cretaceous in Colorado Plateau: American Association of Petroleum Geologists Bulletin, v. 36, no. 9, p. 1766–1776.

Tschudy, R.H., Tschudy, B.D., and Craig, L.C., 1984, Palynological evaluation of Cedar Mountain and Burro Canyon Formations, Colorado Plateau: U.S. Geological Survey Professional Paper 1281, 21 p.

Willis, B.J., 1998, Permeability structure of a compound valley fill in the Cretaceous Fall River Formation of South Dakota: American Association of Petroleum Geologists Bulletin, v. 82, p. 206–227.

Willis, B.J., and White, C.D., 2000, Quantitative outcrop data for flow simulation: Journal of Sedimentary Research, v. 70, p. 788–802.

Young, R.G., 1960, Dakota Group of Colorado Plateau: American Association of Petroleum Geologists Bulletin, v. 44, no. 2, p. 156–194.